Getting THE Call for Job Interviews and Offers

GETTING THE CALL

Executive Coach Reveals Job Searching SECRETS Employer's Don't Want You to Know.

Volume 8, 4th Edition

To

THE CAREER POTENTIAL SERIES

By

EDWARD J. MURPHY

CAREER MAKER PUBLISHING

Discover the Job Searching SECRETS Employer's Don't Want You to Know.

Copyright © 2012

By

THE CAREER MAKER

Published by Career Maker Publishing

10240 E. Tillman Avenue

Mesa, AZ 85212

816.347.0591

ISBN-13: 978-1480257900

ISBN-10: 1480257907

BISAC: Business & Economics / Careers / Job Hunting

All rights reserved. No part of this book may be reproduced or transmitted in any form or by any means, electronic or mechanical, including photocopying, recording, or by any information storage and retrieval system, without the written permission of Career Maker Publishing, except where permitted by law.

The information presented herein represents the views of the author as of the date of publication. This book is presented for informational purposes only. Due to the rate at which conditions change, the author reserves the right to alter and update his opinions at any time. While every attempt has been made to verify the information in this book, the author does not assume any responsibility for errors, inaccuracies, or omissions.

WHAT OTHERS SAY ABOUT
EDWARD J. MURPHY

"I thought I could write a wonderful resume until I had your assistance in preparing a better resume to replace it. I thought I knew how to find a position with a company until you showed me 19 ways to do it. I thought I could handle almost any question until you showed me how wrong I was. I thought I did not need any job interview role-play exercises until you critiqued the results of my videotaped interview. Luck is when preparation meets opportunity. You prepared me and gave me the opportunity to prove my worth to a company. That means you are my luck."

- Roy P., Bellevue, WA

"Ed was tremendously instrumental in directing and assisting the implementation of my career search. It was through his dogged persistence, guidance and genuine encouragement that kept me on track and lead me to the successful position of receiving multiple offers accepting an offer from ...corporation. This was all done in 60 days. Ed was always available when I needed clarification of what I was doing, with recommendations and suggestions as to how to maximize my efforts."

- Jim S. Rancho Santa Fe, CA

"I have appreciated your candor, inspiration, insight and practical experience. I have found your goal identification exercises, negotiation skills, and personal growth strategies particularly useful both personally and professionally. I would most heartily recommend your services as a personal coach to anyone who has high moral character, is intrinsically motivated, and has a desire to be the best they can be."

- Cliff J., Kansas City, MO

I DEDICATE THIS BOOK

TO

My *Nephew,*

ROBERT "ROB" CHASE

"Rob, thank you for all you've done to help me. You have truly risen to the level of your potential. I am so proud of all you've accomplished in your lifetime, especially in raising such a wonderful family. Continue to use your talents in the service of others and you will find true joy and peace in this life and in the next. Know that I love you always."

TABLE OF CONTENTS

INTRODUCTION 7

CHAPTER 1: WHAT EVERY COMPANY MUST DO TO SURVIVE 11

CHAPTER 2: WHAT VALUE DO YOU BRING TO AN EMPLOYER? 19

CHAPTER 3: WHAT ARE YOUR ASSETS AND LIABILITIES? 23

CHAPTER 4: WHAT'S YOUR SEARCH FOCUS? 27

CHAPTER 5: ASSESSING YOUR CURRENT RESUME 33

CHAPTER 6: BUILDING YOUR COMPELLING RESUME 41

CHAPTER 7: 19+ PROVEN WAYS TO GET THE INTERVIEW 53

CHAPTER 8: INTERVIEWING TO RECEIVE THE JOB OFFER 73

CHAPTER 9: NEGOTIATING TO RECEIVE THE HIGHEST OFFER 95

CHAPTER 10: ASSESSING YOUR JOB SEARCH 115

CHAPTER 11: CHANGING CAREERS? 121

ACKNOWLEDGEMENTS 125

ABOUT THE FOUNDER 127

OTHER BOOKS 129

INDEX 133

Discover the Job Searching SECRETS Employer's Don't Want You to Know.

INTRODUCTION

> *"Keep interested in your career, however humble;*
> *it is a real possession in the changing fortunes of time.*
> *- Desiderata*

This book is about *Getting THE Call for Job Interviews and Offers* and focuses on how to create a compelling resume strong enough to generate a phone call, how to get your resume in front of the right people, how to interview strong enough to be selected as the #1 candidate, and how to negotiate strong enough to receive the highest offer the employer can afford.

There's nothing more stressful than trying to conduct a job search - after losing your job. I've been there!

It's a SCARY Time!

You have no cash flow and you're surviving on savings and help from friends and family. The fear and uncertainty of when you'll be reemployed are crushing on you and your family. The biggest frustration is the Silence; your phone never rings - even after weeks and months of effort.

You've done everything you know how to do and nothing so far has worked. The fear of the unknown, the embarrassment, the lack of self-worth and self-doubt are mounting. You're desperate and ready to take any job just to support your family.

How much longer can you continue your insane behavior; doing the same thing, over and over again, while expecting a different result? There has to be a better way! Well there is and it's time for a change – this is why I wrote this book. I can help you!

One of my clients said it best when he wrote,

> *"Thanks to Ed, I learned the secrets of running a successful job search and in only two weeks I found my career position. I actually had two offers from which to choose and was able to leverage that situation to a 10% raise plus a bonus, all before I ever worked a day. Thanks doesn't seem enough."* – William S., San Diego, CA

I bring over 21 years of experience as an Executive Coach, helping hundreds of people, from recent college graduates to CEO's, find meaningful employment. I worked for four of the largest consulting, outplacement and e-cruiting companies in America in Seattle, San Diego, and Kansas City. It was here that I learned the secrets of making my client's phone ring.

Without a phone call – your search is dead!

To make your phone ring you'll need a compelling resume; one that speaks in a language every employer understands and sells your potential.

This book is unique because it:

- Comes from my personal struggles finding employment and the struggles of my clients over a 15-year period
- Teaches you specifically what employers are looking for
- Helps you write and speak in a language every employer understands
- Includes all the things you want to know and the top things you didn't realize you needed to know
- And, much, much, more!

Everything in this book has worked for me, worked for my clients, and I know they'll work for you!

One thing I know for certain, sitting home and waiting for your phone to ring, is the definition of complacency, which will kill your job search and your career.

Stop wishing you were better and do something about it today!

Also, if you feel this information could help someone else, please take a few moments to let them know. If it turns out to make a difference in their life, they'll be forever grateful to you – as will I.

Let's make a difference together - one person at a time!

All the best!

Ed

Founder of *TheCAREERMaker.com*
Coauthor of *The Effectiveness Guide*
email: *ed.murphy77@gmail.com*

Note: Marked in **Segoe Print** throughout this book, you'll find *Takeaways* or *Key Points* which summarize the main message we wish to convey.

You're not just looking for a job, you're looking for a place for your CAREER to happen.

Discover the Job Searching SECRETS Employer's Don't Want You to Know.

CHAPTER 1:
WHAT EVERY COMPANY MUST DO TO SURVIVE

> *"Never take your eyes off the cash flow because it's the life blood of business."*
> - Richard Branson's 21 Survival Strategies for Small Business Success

Have you ever struggled trying to determine what's most important and what's not; especially when there are too many things to do and too few people and hours in the day to get it all done?

To survive requires focus and prioritization. Many new employers let their employer decide what's most important because they fear making a mistake. However, small business owners, entrepreneurs, and consultants don't have this luxury. Here's a methodology to help ensure your focus and priorities are clear to help you survive.

Here, we'll be examining both Private-Sector Corporations like Microsoft and Public-Sector Organizations like School Districts and Government Agencies, to better understand what's most important to their survival.

What matters most to the survival of PRIVATE-SECTOR CORPORATIONS?

Have you ever struggled trying to figure out what matters most? If not, you will. Especially, when there are too many things to do and too few people and hours in the day to get it all done. Well, it all comes down to Focus and Priority. But how can you focus or prioritize without knowing what matters most? This is why we'll be examining Private-Sector Corporations like Microsoft to better understand what matters most to their survival.

As an Executive Coach, I often asked senior executives from Private-Sector Companies, "What matters most to the survival of your company?" The first answer I normally got was People. And, people are an important resource, but not the most important resource. Just quit your job and see how quickly you'll be replaced. Some said Technology, which is important, but again, not the most important. So, what really matters most? The only people who don't struggle with this question are Small Business Owners. These guys get it.

Any small business owner will tell you that the correct answer is Positive Cash Flow (or PCF).

Without PCF, the company can't pay their bills and they're soon out-of-business. Without PCF, the company's bankrupt. Game over! And, according to the Small Business Administration, this is the primary reason why 80% of start-up companies fail within their first 3 years. But what about your business unit? If you can link what you and your business unit do for your company's PCF and how it has improved or achieved better results, your business unit is essential to your company.

In the same vein, if your business unit can't be directly linked to one or more of the activities that generate PCF, your unit could be considered non-essential and therefore expendable - not a place you want to stay for long. So, what activities generate *Positive Cash Flow*?

What Generates PCF?

Here are the four most important activities that generate *Positive Cash Flow* for Private-Sector companies like Microsoft:

- **Increase Revenues:** To increase revenues from the sale of products and services normally involves those in sales, marketing, sales support, business development, or strategic development. Can you find and recommend new and innovative ways to sell more products or services like any of these activities? Bringing in new customers, selling more to the same customers, discovering new uses for old products, or finding new ways to bring more money in the door, are how revenues are increased.

- **Decrease Operating Costs:** Decreasing operating costs, or saving money, is everyone's job. Can you find and recommend new and innovative ways to reduce costs like any of these activities: consolidating, eliminating, cost sharing, getting a better price from a supplier, conserving, saving time or being more effective, efficient, and consistent? Because this is how Operating Costs are decreased.

- **Better Use of Available Resources:** Everyone's job is to better use the resources they already have. Can you find and recommend new and innovative ways to better use the resources your company already has like any of these activities: streamlining, eliminating redundancies, consolidating, conserving, waste reduction, process improvement, reducing time required, becoming more efficient, doing more with less, better maintaining equipment and vehicles to extend their service life and finding quicker or easier ways of doing things. And how much money or time could be saved annually? Because this is how to better use the resources of your company.

- **Anticipate Problems Today to Save Money Tomorrow:** Anticipating problems today to save money tomorrow is also everyone's job.

Discover the Job Searching SECRETS Employer's Don't Want You to Know.

Since law suits are very expensive, can you find and recommend new and innovative ways to anticipate problems today to save money tomorrow like any of these activities: creating important policies and procedures, creating better contracts, ensuring the right insurance is in force, ensuring compliance with outside agencies, creating better physical and cyber security procedures, creating better property accountability procedures, or eliminating unsafe conditions. This is what saves money tomorrow by anticipating problems today.

How can you best use this knowledge?

If you work for a Private-Sector Company like Microsoft, your career depends on your ability to identify, measure, and increase your value added (individual productivity and sustainability) to one or more of the four activities that contribute to PCF.

This step only pertains to half the Job Market. What about all those who are not profit driven like nurses, teachers, fireman, and all those who put themselves in harm's way every day to defend us and keep us safe? Not every organization is profit driven. So, how do they identify, measure and increase their value add?

What matters most to the survival of PUBLIC SECTOR ORGANIZATIONS?

Since these organizations do not focus on profit generation, what matters most to them is providing a service that serves the greater good (like schools and government agencies).

Public-Sector Organizations use what is called a Band Of Excellence (BOE) to measure and assess their level of services.

For those who work in the Public-Sector, like teachers or government workers, they are required to achieve, maintain, or exceed the *Band Of Excellence (BOE)* set by their organization. So, what is a *Band Of Excellence?*

Getting THE Call for Job Interviews and Offers

Band Of Excellence:

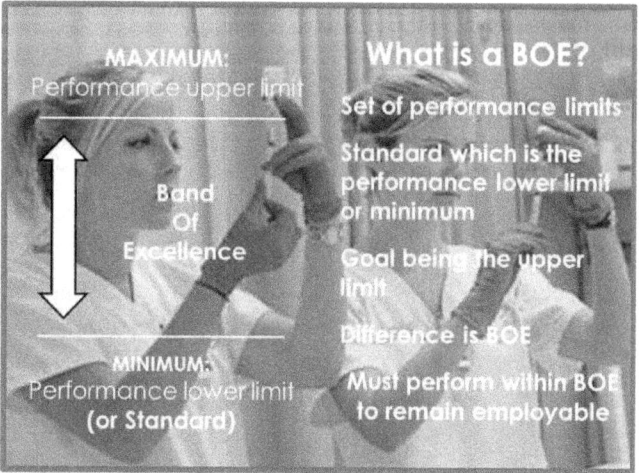

A *Band Of Excellence (BOE)* is a set of performance limits ranging from the Minimum (The Standard) - being the performance lower limit and the Maximum - being the performance upper limit. And the difference between the Minimum and the Maximum is called the *Band Of Excellence*. If your performance stays within the *Band Of Excellence*, you remain employable.

And, here's a simple example.

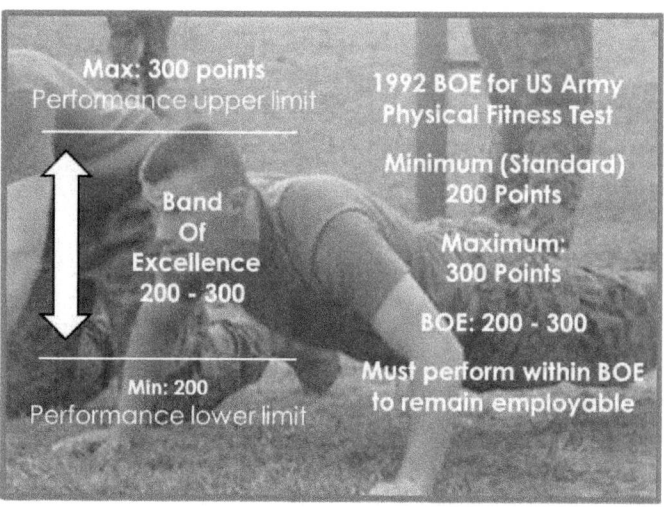

The biggest government agency on the planet is the US Department of Defense. In 1992, as a former US Army Officer, here's the BOE all soldiers used when taking Annual Physical Fitness Test.

The BOE Minimum (or Standard) was 200 points overall. The BOE Maximum was 300 points overall. The BOE was 200 - 300 for the test overall to remain promotable. If a Soldier failed to achieve 200 points overall, he was retrained and re-tested. If he failed a second time, he was considered un-promotable and administratively processed for release from the military.

How does this apply to the Business World?

Let's take teachers and government workers as an example. To remain employable, they're continuously assessed by their supervisors using assessment standards for specific job tasks and behaviors. Employers use these activities to assess both individual and unit performance against their BOEs.

Public-Sector BOEs are measured by daily observations, customer feedback, certification, performance reviews, external audits, visits, compliance inspections, annual qualification, and even continuing education.

How is Performance Measured?

BOE's are used to measure and assess both individual and unit performance, which includes results, behavior, and potential. If each follower continues to meet their BOE Standards, they remain employable. If not, they are retrained, retested and either put on probation, reinstated, or released. And, if they achieve, maintain, or exceed their BOE Maximums, they should expect some form of recognition.

BOE's are needed to measure excellence in Public-Sector Organizations because they're not driven by *Positive Cash Flow*. They are used to make periodic assessments to determine if individuals, units, and systems have achieved, maintained, or exceeded their BOEs. Without a BOE, you can't measure performance or even tell if you're improving or getting worse.

BOEs are also used by Private-Sector Corporations to help generate Positive Cash Flow.

How are BOEs Created?

To create any Public-Sector Organization, it must go through these three phases:

Phase 1: Must serve the greater good (schools or government agencies)

Phase 2: Must create a BOE to maintain or enhance that service

Phase 3: Must consistently achieve, maintain, or exceed their BOE

This is how they maintain the funding needed to operate, which comes from city, state, and federal tax revenues. And, if the organization can no longer meet their BOE Standards for services, they run the risk of losing their funding.

If you work for a Public-Sector Organization, like school districts or government agencies, your career depends on your ability to identify, measure, and increase your BOE value added.

Summary: The two things every company in the world must have to survive:

- *Private-Sector Companies* (like Microsoft and all other *For Profit* Companies) must generate PCF and achieve, maintain, or exceed their BOEs.

- *Public-Sector Organizations* (like School Districts) must achieve, maintain, or exceed their BOEs and receive external funding.

Employer's think and speak PCF/BOE.
It's that simple-don't screw it up!

Discover the Job Searching SECRETS Employer's Don't Want You to Know.

CHAPTER 2:
WHAT VALUE DO YOU BRING TO AN EMPLOYER?

"Price is what you pay. Value is what you get."
- *Warren Buffett*

Now that you know that employers speak and think PCF/BOE, how can you make your resume speak PCF/BOE? To figure that out, let's first identify your "value added".

To identify your *value added*, here are the most important questions to ask to determine how you're linked to PCF/BOE. Answering these questions will help you determine how you (and your business unit) are linked to the things that matter most: contributing to your Leader's PCF/BOE goals. So, let's review each, one at a time.

How do you contribute to your Leader's PCF/BOE goals?

Here's a true story.

> *One day, Bob was called for a job interview for a job that he really wanted. This new job came with a promotion and doubled his salary. You know the drill; this is where you get the opportunity to justify your existence to complete strangers.*

As expected, Bob was nervous, especially when the interviewer started out by asking him, "Why should we hire you?

After Bob picked himself up off the floor, he stammered something that most people would say, "Well, I was responsible for...."

Then, to make things worse, the interviewer interrupted him and said, "Stop! No one cares what you were responsible for. I want to know what you achieved. What got better because you were there? What was your value added (individual productivity and sustainability) to your leader?"

Unfortunately, Bob didn't get the job, which was a shame because he was the best of all of those they interviewed.

He just didn't know his value added.
Bob didn't know how to sell himself.

This story unfortunately is the norm rather than the exception. All too often good people have no clue what's most important to a potential leader or how to articulate their value added. Has this ever happened to you? If not, it will. But, by reading this guide, you'll never hesitate to answer these questions.

Your value added is quite simply the sum of everything you bring to the table (like your knowledge, skills, experience, achievements, attitude, relationships, character, and balance) that has contributed, in some measurable and significant way, to the achievement of your leader's goals.

You already know how important it is to your career to be able to add value to your leader. But, did you know that most people have no clue how to do that. The problem comes from the fact that few people truly understand what matters most to the survival of their organization.

Once you learn how to identify, measure and increase your value added to your leader, you're well on the way to becoming absolutely essential.

Most people only begin to identify their value added near the end of their career, if at all. To identify your value added (individual productivity and sustainability), here are the most important questions to ask to determine how you're linked to PCF/BOE. Answering these questions will help you determine how you (and your business unit) are linked to the things that matter most: contributing to your leader's PCF/BOE goals. So, let's review each one.

How do you contribute to your Leader's PCF/BOE Goals?

It all starts out with a few assumptions. The first assumption is that you know your leader's goals. If not, ask. Second assumption is that your leader's goals are measurable. And the third assumption is that you (or your unit) contribute directly to your leader's PCF/BOE goals.

What do you (or your business unit) do (what duties do you perform)?

Are your duties essential to the survival of your company? How do you help others and who are you helping? What are you doing to better help others? Most followers don't deal directly with customers. Most often, your #1 customer will be another follower or unit within your company.

What are your PCF/BOE Standards to achieve, maintain, or exceed?

What's the *Band of Excellence?* How do you contribute to your leader's PCF/BOE Goals? Standards here mean the minimum acceptable level of performance (results and behavior). This includes the stated, inherent, and expected standards for the duties you perform. Where's the line between the acceptable and unacceptable? What does your leader and organization expect of your performance (results and behavior)?

How does your Leader measure this?

How does your leader measure your performance (results and behavior)? Who does the measuring? What are the metrics and how often does your leader make assessments?

How does your performance compare to your peers?

Compare to your peers means compare yourself to those at your level within your organization. What are they doing to become better?

While this is not the best method for comparison, it's important to collaborate with your peers - because you'll learn a lot.

How does your performance compare to a year ago?

The best way to measure your performance is to compare yourself to where you were a year ago.

Are you getting better over time?

Are you getting better or worse? How do you know for sure? Who is counting or measuring? What are the metrics? If so, how much better? Without measuring and keeping track of how you're doing, how can you ever answer this question?

What do you get for being the best or for improving?

Are there incentives in place for continuous excellent performance? Have you received awards, promotions, raises, accolades, kudos, or other recognition? Do you have copies of this recognition? What was the recognition for? What did you do to earn it?

If you're not improving, guess what your peers are doing?

This also includes professional development, which means additional education, training, and certifications.

What improved because you were there?

From the first day you started, until today, what have you done or recommended to be done that got better because you were there? What was your contribution to moving the work forward? What have you done to make your performance more effective, efficient, and consistent?

Answering these questions will help you determine how you (and your unit) are linked to the things that matter most: your leader's PCF/BOE goals.

CHAPTER 3:
WHAT ARE YOUR ASSETS AND LIABILITIES?

"I have no particular talent. I am merely inquisitive."
— Albert Einstein

Before learning how to identify your assets and liabilities, it's important to understand a few important warnings.

Warning #1: Don't quit your job unless you have a guaranteed better job to move too. If you quit, you lose two valuable things; unemployment insurance and severance.

Warning #2: Don't fall into the trap of waiting until your unemployment insurance and/or severance runs out before starting your search. It could take you at least one-month for each $10,000 in the pay you're seeking before you find a new position, or longer. Always be looking for a better opportunity even after you become reemployed!

Warning #3: Don't take your foot off the job search accelerator! Just because one opportunity looks good, don't slow down your search. At the last minute, this good opportunity could disappear and you'll be left with nothing, feeling demoralized. Don't stop your search actions until the day after your first day at your new job.

Identify your Assets

Let's take an inventory of your assets. Your assets are your knowledge, skills, experience, attitude, achievements, relationships, and balance. This is what you bring to the table. This is what you're selling - your potential!

Here are the Asset Categories:

- Knowledge: What knowledge do you have? Have you been tested and found worthy? What is your level of educational, certification, license, and special training?
- Skills: What can you do with your knowledge? What're your transferrable skills? What can you do to enhance your employer's results?
- Experience: What different environments (locations, industries, sectors, level, functional areas, size of company, Fortune 1000 companies) have you been in and how long?
- Achievements: How well did you (or your team) perform? What did you accomplish? What got better because you were there? How did it improve your employer's results? What obstacles did you overcome?
- Character: How do you treat others? True character is right behavior; what you say and do when no one's around including traits like Adaptable, Dependable, Integrity, Judgment, Loyalty, Moral Courage, Positive Attitude, Drive and Respect.
- Relationships: How well do you work with others? What would others say about your people skills? Have you ever led a team? What drives you crazy? What's important in your relationship with your Leader? Who do you know that can help us?
- Balance: How balanced is your life overall? Is there anything in your life that is out of balance that could become a distraction to your career later? If you're out of balance, this could be a liability.

This is what you're selling - so make it count!

Your job during the interview is to increase the perceived value of your assets. Your assets are what produce results for the employer lucky enough to have you on their team.

Identify your Liabilities

Social networking (LinkedIn, Facebook, and Twitter could be a liability. 50% of employers admit checking social networking sites before making a hiring decision. Because of this, don't post information concerning politics, religion, sex, or humor (includes content and photos). If they're already there, remove them!

Other liabilities include:

- No GED, High School, or College
- No training in the industry
- No computer skills
- No experience in the industry or function
- Appearance: Poor hygiene, overweight, smoker, poor health
- Bad credit, criminal record (Felony DUI)
- Age: Too old or too young; Lack of experience
- Inability to communicate your transferable skills
- Over qualified (too much education and/or experience)
- Being out of work too long, gaps in your resume
- Been in three companies in the past five years
- Bad performance reviews
- Lack of good references

As you assess your liabilities, prepare to respond to each during an interview.

Being prepared is vital to your success.

Discover the Job Searching SECRETS Employer's Don't Want You to Know.

CHAPTER 4:
WHAT'S YOUR SEARCH FOCUS?

"Don't be afraid to give your best to what seemingly are small jobs. Every time you conquer one it makes you that much stronger. If you do the little jobs well, the big ones will tend to take care of themselves."
- Dale Carnegie

Your search focus is critically important. Without it, you'll just be a wandering generality.

How do Employers Fill Vacancies?

Because time is critical, employers normally fill vacant positions by;

- *Selecting someone from within their company*
- *Asking for referrals from their employees*
- *Asking for referrals from family, friends, and associates*

- And, as a last resort, they create a job requisition (including the duties and responsibilities, minimum prerequisites, and desired skills) to begin the hiring process which could take several weeks (if not months)

Special Note: Notice that many positions are filled from referrals from others. These positions won't be advertised. This is important because it shapes your actions during your search! You can only access them by using the techniques presented in this guide.

How do People Find Jobs?

Most people find jobs through word of mouth referrals and by contacting companies directly. However, all these sources produce results.

- ***Word of mouth - 35%***
- ***Contacting companies - 30%***
- Ads and internet - 14%
- Agencies and recruiters - 11%
- Referrals from schools, unions, trade journals, and civil services tests – 10%

Special Note: Notice that **65% of positions** come from word of mouth and contacting companies. These positions won't be advertised. This is important because it shapes your actions during your search! You can ONLY access them by using the techniques presented in this guide.

What's the Role of Human Resources?

When applying for a posted job your resume will go directly to the Human Resources (HR) Office. This process could generate hundreds, if not thousands, of resumes. HR will screen all the resumes and select a few to send to a hiring manager. If the hiring manager likes what he sees, he will ask HR to schedule an interview.

This is the traditional hiring process (if the hiring manager can't find a replacement through referrals). As a result, this traditional process doesn't put the odds in your favor. You need a better way of getting your resume in front of the right people. This is why I wrote this guide.

Getting THE Call for Job Interviews and Offers

To create your search focus, let's first create your 30-Second Commercial.

Create your 30-Second Commercial

Your 30-Second Commercial is nothing more than your answer to the question, "What do you do?"

How do most unemployed people answer this question? Most people would say, Well, I've been laid off, fired, or downsized, or I'm doing some free-lance work, or I'm between positions, or whatever.

That kind of answer is not only bad self-talk, but it causes the person you're speaking to - to want to change the subject. So why put yourself in that awkward position. Instead, give a quick overview of your career by telling them how you've helped other people.

Your 30-Second Commercial should answer these questions:

- How do you see yourself (Title/Function)? I've been the...
- What have you done to improve business?
- How much experience do you have in which industries?
- What are you seeking?

When you practice your 30-second commercial in the mirror daily, ask yourself if the person in the mirror is articulate, enthusiastic and focused? If not, keep doing it until you are. This will prepare you for game-time, when you get to do it for real.

Remember: your potential is the product you're selling. Make your 30-Second Commercial count.

Sample 30-Second Commercial for someone who is UNEMPLOYED:

I've been the Director of Finance for several Fortune 500 companies in the Seattle and Kansas City area, where I managed a division of 45 associates. I helped save my employer $1.5 million recently converting our accounting functions over to a state-of-the-art software operation. I've spent the last 15+ years in the high technology manufacturing industry. I'm currently on an active search for a senior financial opportunity here in Kansas City.

Sample 30-Second Commercial for someone who is EMPLOYED:

> *I'm the Director of Finance for a Fortune 500 company here in the Kansas City area, where I manage a division of 45 associates. I recently save my employer $1.5 million converting our accounting functions over to a state-of-the-art software operation. I've spent the last 15+ years in the high technology manufacturing industry. I'm currently seeking a new CFO/Director of Finance opportunity here in Kansas City. (Be prepared to explain why?)*

The trick here is to prepare your commercial and to practice it several times every day in the mirror. The practice is designed to ensure you can deliver your message with enthusiasm, focus and clarity.

The only way you'll know is to watch yourself in the mirror. If there is no enthusiasm, do it until you're enthusiastic. Practice every day so that you're fully prepared.

<u>Remember:</u> There's no such thing as magic or luck here. You make your own luck every day. You just can't see it.

Luck is when preparation meets opportunity.

Opportunities are all around you. Either you didn't notice or you were unprepared or both. Now, you'll be more prepared for a real opportunity.

What's your Search Focus?

Spend some quality time deciding what you're looking for - your Focus. Describe your ideal job.

Here are the components to creating a good Focus Statement:

- <u>Title</u>: Project Manager, Technical Analyst?
- <u>Level</u>: Entry, supervisor, manager, director, VP, C-level?
- <u>Function</u>: Sales, Marketing, Operations, Finance, Research?
- <u>Type</u>: Full-time, Part-time, Contract, Consulting?
- <u>Industry</u>: Aerospace, Defense, Automotive, Agriculture?
- <u>Location</u>: Open to relocation? How long a commute? Sales territory?

- Compensation: Range of desired pay? Other benefits?
- Leadership or technical: Lead people or manage things-accounts?
- Target Companies: List 10 companies you'd like to work for?
- Deal Stoppers: Like certain industries, 100% travel, foreign travel, exposure to danger, multi-level, sales, insurance, or work weekends?

Can you have more than one Focus?

Sure, but be careful! Now, you've defused your time and effort in your search. We have no problem with a dual Focus. But, any more than that, we don't recommend.

Discover the Job Searching SECRETS Employer's Don't Want You to Know.

CHAPTER 5:
ASSESSING YOUR CURRENT RESUME

"Resume: a written exaggeration of only the good things a person has done in the past, as well as a wish list of the qualities a person would like to have." - Bo Bennett

You've previously learned how *Positive Cash Flow (PCF)* and *Band Of Excellence (BOE)* relate to every employer on the planet. That's how your resume should read.

It must be abundantly clear to the reader what you've done previously to help your employer with his PCF/BOE goals. If not, why would any employer waste his time interviewing you? He wouldn't! A PCF/BOE rich resume is what gets you the phone call. From then on, speak PCF/BOE during both phone interviews and in person.

<u>Scenario:</u> I'll now take you through the exact process I took my last client through to create his compelling resume. His name was John Brown. Before I started, I asked John for a copy of his resume. I assumed that his resume was a Good resume, at least to him.

Discover the Job Searching SECRETS Employer's Don't Want You to Know.

STEP 1

Even though John had sixteen years of great experience, and just got his Master's degree in Architecture, his resume (below) was in bad shape.

John Brown

1111 Windsor Drive, Summit Mills, al 68654; 913.123.9876; bobo@gmail.com

Objective: to become an arkitect in a chalenging envirment

2004-Present: John's Home Improvement Company, al – Owner, made home repairs

2002-2004: Schmidt Construction, wa – Construction Superintindant, managed several project

1994-2002: Albertsons Food Store, ca - Asistant Store Manager, assisted store managr in running the store

Education: Bachelor and Master in Arkitecture from alabama U

Refrences:

Ted Brown: 213.345.221

Joe Smith: 213.436.278

Ralph Burns: 213.45.6657

I was stunned by the quality of his resume, especially the misspellings, but I offered no critique at first. My only goal was to move his resume from being Good to being Better. I just set it aside and began to ask John the following questions, while I took notes.

Without looking at your resume, record your answers to the following questions. then, compare your answers to your current resume and we'll see if there's a difference.

STEP 2

Here are the questions I asked John.

Have you ever helped an Employer...?

Make more money by:

    Selling more products or services?

    Bringing in new customers?

    Selling more to the same customers?

    Discovering new uses for an old product?

    Finding new ways to bring more money in the door?

Save money by:

    Consolidating?

    Eliminating?

    Getting a better price from a supplier?

    Being more efficient?

    Conserving?

    Saving time?

Better use of what they already have by:

    Streamlining?

    Process improvement?

    Reducing time required?

    Becoming more efficient or doing more with less?

    Better maintaining to extend service life?

    Finding a better, quicker, or easier way?

Solve problems today to save $$$ tomorrow by:
    Creating important policies and procedures?
    Creating better contracts?
    Managing risk better?
    Ensuring the right insurance is in force?
    Ensuring compliance with outside agencies?
    Creating better physical and cyber security procedures?
    Creating better property accountability procedures?
    Eliminating unsafe conditions?

Meet or exceed the Band Of Excellence?
    What do you do (What function did it perform)?
    What *Band Of Excellence* did you have to meet or exceed?
    How did your Leader measure this?

How did your work compare to others or to previous years?
    How did your results compare to others?
    How did your results compare to previous years?
    Are you getting better over time?
    What did your Leader give you for being the best or for improving?
    What got better because you were there?

What work experience are you most proud?
    Brag a little!
    Make more money or save money?
    Better use what they already have?
    Solve problems today to save $$$ tomorrow?
    Achieve, sustain, or exceed your BOE?
    Most difficult task?

Best results?

Write down your story!

Why are you leaving out the details?

How important was this task you're proud of?

How many people were involved?

How complicated was the task?

How much money was involved?

Were you on a tight time deadline?

With whom did you have to coordinate?

Was there any risk of failure?

If it wasn't easy, tell me why?

Why're you so proud of this?

Have you ever supervised the efforts of others?

How many?

Who were they?

What was the problem?

What actions were taken by you or your team?

What were the quantifiable results?

How difficult was this task and why?

Don't leave out the details!

How complex was the task?

How big was the budget?

What obstacles did you have to overcome?

How difficult was it?

Talk gross, total annual cost?

How many people were involved (directly/indirectly)?

What were the consequences of failure?

Have you ever:

    Led? Managed? Directed?

    Supervised?

    Coordinated?

    Facilitated?

Why would anyone want to hire you?

    What do you bring to the table?

    What would others say about you?

    Can you be counted on to produce excellent results?

    Don't leave out the details!

What do you do best?

    Received favorable comments?

    Receive praise?

    People came to you for advice or help?

    Received awards or special recognition?

    What're your special gifts?

    What gets you out of bed in the morning?

After asking these questions, I had two full pages of great material; even though I had to drag it out of John – kicking and screaming! I then asked John, why wasn't all this in your resume? He just stared at me with his mouth open. I again asked, why did you leave it out? Again, silence and a dumb look on his face.

The sad truth is that most people have no clue how valuable they are to a potential employer.

I then asked the killer question, *"John, how does this make you feel?"* He was obviously stunned by what had just happened. It took a while for it to sink in and he finally said, *"Wow! I had no idea all that should be in my resume."*

Still think your resume's great? This may help explain why you're not getting called for interviews. Your resume is just not compelling enough to generate the call.

What's a "Compelling" Resume?

Think of your resume as a movie trailer. Is your movie trailer exciting enough to make someone want to see the movie? Is your resume compelling enough for someone to want to know more? Does your resume show your contributions to your Leader's PCF/BOE goals, the solutions and full range of skills you bring, or how your transferrable skills apply to any industry?

If not, then why would any employer in their right mind want to waste their time talking to you? Do a better job of selling your knowledge, skills, experience, achievements, attitude, and relationships than you've done in the past!

With the two full pages of notes I took from questioning John, I now had great *Positive Cash Flow* content that I could add to his Good resume to make it Better. However, my next goal was to take his resume from Better to Best.

Note: When building your resume, don't tell me what you were responsible for – no one cares! Instead, tell me what you, or your team, actually accomplished, finished, or made happen. What got better because you were there?

STEP 3

What follows in the next chapter is the exact process I used to produce the best compelling resume possible for John to make his phone ring more frequently.

Discover the Job Searching SECRETS Employer's Don't Want You to Know.

CHAPTER 6: BUILDING YOUR COMPELLING RESUME

"Do not be too timid and squeamish about your actions. All life is an experiment." - Ralph Waldo Emerson

Any Compelling Resume consists of these seven levels:

LEVEL 1: HEADING

I started building John's new resume, from top to bottom, one level at a time.

John Brown

1111 Windsor Drive, Summit Mills, AL 68654; 913.123.9876; jbrown@gmail.com

If your email address is loverboy@xyz.com, go to Yahoo or Google and sign up for a free email address with your name only. You want to project a professional image. Details matter!

Boldface and enlarge your name to make it stand out. Use a phone number that you'll actually answer and change your voicemail to a more professional message, if necessary.

LEVEL 2: POSITION TITLES

I asked John what position title he was seeking (right from his Focus Statement). He wanted to be a Design and Build Architect.

Design and Build Architect

Most resumes have an Objective paragraph, which doesn't specifically state what you want to do. These titles come from your search Focus Statement. Clearly state what you want to do. Don't let the reader guess what you want to do.

LEVEL 3: KEY WORDS FOR SCANNING

Since John had no clue what his key words might be, I did a quick web search for a generic job description of an Architect. Key words can also be assumed, if you know the industry. If you were the employer, what would you be seeking?

Ensure you own these key words because the employer will verify that you do. Keywords tend to be nouns that are industry-specific qualifications, skills, or terms. Some keywords include degrees or certifications, job titles, computer lingo, industry jargon, product names, company names and professional organizations. You can also identify keywords by visiting company websites and reviewing job postings.

Employers often search job banks looking for resumes with key words or requirements specific to their job description. Including more keywords throughout your online resume will increase your chances of being identified as a potential match. Also, use keywords in any description of yourself which most job sites require.

Getting THE Call for Job Interviews and Offers

Be careful with Acronyms and Abbreviations:

Every industry has their own unique set of jargon, acronyms, and abbreviations; the special language that only industry insiders understand. Unfortunately, not everyone reading your resume will understand them, especially if you're applying for positions outside your industry. A good rule is to always define your jargon, acronym, or abbreviation the first time it appears in any document.

As an example, in John's original resume he had ICF and SIP. In his final resume, you'll find Insulated Concrete Forms (ICF), and Structure Insulated Panel Systems (SIPS).

How important is the Job Description?

There are two types of job descriptions; the generic job description from a web search to give you key words for adding to your resume and the employer's specific job description found in job postings (which is used for applying for posted positions and for interviewing). From searching the web for Architect Job Description, I found the following generic job description:

> *Researches, plans, designs, and administers building projects for clients, applying knowledge of design, construction procedures, zoning and building codes, and building materials: Consults with client to determine functional and spatial requirements of new structure or renovation, and prepares information regarding design, specifications, materials, color, equipment, estimated costs, and construction time.*
>
> *Plans layout of project and integrates engineering elements into unified design for client review and approval.*
>
> *Prepares scale drawings and contract documents for building contractors. Represents client in obtaining bids and awarding construction contracts. Administers construction contracts and conducts periodic on-site observation of work during construction to monitor compliance with plans. May prepare operating and maintenance manuals, studies, and reports. May use computer-assisted design software and equipment to prepare project designs and plans. May direct activities of workers engaged in preparing drawings and specification documents.*

Do you really own your Key Word?

My next step was to sit down with John and asked him which key words (bolded) from the above job description truthfully belonged to him. I told him that during the interview, the employer would attempt to verify if he truly owned those key words.

To prove that you own them you'll need some form of documentation (diploma, certificate, transcripts, and past performance reviews), or a great story to tell to convince them, or a personal reference from your past that can confirm your resume

John carefully selected about 30% of the key words from the job description. I then added them to John's key words, Level 3. In the end, these are the key words that John could easily substantiate.

This is what it looked like when I added it to his Compelling Resume:

Project / Project Manager / Plan / Design / Coordinate / Estimate Costs / Administer / Construction / Architecture / Architect / Engineer / Scale Drawings / Contracts / Client Review / Obtain Bid / Award Contract / Monitor Compliance / On-site Observation / CAD / Prepare Drawings / Zoning / Building Code

LEVEL 4: MARKETING SUMMARY

At this point, I began to write John's compelling marketing summary. The purpose of this paragraph is to entice the reader to read the entire resume. I took the information from his resume (not much help) and from the two pages of notes I took earlier (as part of his resume assessment questions) and this is what I created.

> *Career professional with a Master's degree in Architecture plus sixteen years of experience working with Albertson's, JE Dunn, Turner Construction, Walton, Raul Construction and as a business owner and entrepreneur. Key leadership roles in Food Store Management and the Residential and Commercial Construction industries.*
>
> <u>*Career Track:*</u> *Professional growth as Assistant Store Manager, Construction Superintendent, Entrepreneur, and Home Improvement Business Owner.*

Utilized principle centered leadership in managing multiple projects consisting of technical teams and subcontractors and developing partnerships and programs. Strong track record of increased responsibility, planning, designing, streamlining business processes, with excellent "word-of-mouth" customer satisfaction. Demonstrated entrepreneurial spirit that increased sales and profits.

Proven Record: Skilled at negotiating, estimating, budgeting, scheduling, monitoring compliance, on-site inspections, contracts, and conflict resolution. Consistently exceeded company standards for quality of work and completed requirements on-time, under budget, with excellent client reviews. Completed both a Bachelor's and Master's degree in Architecture at Alabama University concurrent with running his own home improvement business as an entrepreneur, taking 18-21 credit hours per semester.

How many years of experience do you have? Within which industries have you worked? What were your job titles? This is just a snapshot.

Note: I added John's key words (underlined) in this level as well.

LEVEL 5: EDUCATION & TRAINING

This level is straight forward. The only problem I had was clarifying what all his abbreviations meant to the common person; me.

Education and Special Training

Bachelor and Master's Degrees in Architecture from Alabama University, School of Architecture

Computer: Drafting (AutoCAD), Modeling (SketchUp, Revit), Graphics (Photoshop, Illustrator, Indesign), MS Office (Word, Outlook, Excel, and PowerPoint)

Construction: Carpentry (rough and finish), tile work, paint finishes, interior shading systems and floor plans for both spec and custom homes. Knowledgeable of building codes for AL, WA, and CA

Note: I added more key words (underlined) above.

What special knowledge or training do you have that would make you stand out? Most resumes show education and special training last, which often gets overlooked. Here, John's education, computer and construction skills are listed separately and positioned in the middle of the resume (not at the end) to make it stand out more.

Note: The construction paragraph above actually summarizes John's experience and relates directly to architecture.

LEVEL 6: ACHIEVEMENTS AND SKILLS

The information for this level again came from John's resume, my two pages of intake information and a list (below) of the most sought after transferrable skills on the planet.

These are the most sought after Transferrable Skills.

Led, Managed, Directed, Supervised, Coordinated, Facilitated, Administered, Created, Produced, Implemented, Communicated, Introduced, Presented, Planned, Trained, Designed, Engineered, Prepared, Reviewed, Streamlined, Estimated, Solved, Decided, Coached, Mentored, Inspired, Executed, Assessed, and Researched

Based on my 21 years of experience, these are the transferrable skills for which employers pay the most money. After I explained the list to John, I asked him, which transferrable skills do you own? Have you ever used these skills? From this list, he selected the following, which I added to Level 6:

Led, Managed, Supervised, Coordinated, Inspired, Trained, Mentored, Streamlined, Communicated, Solved, Administered and Implemented.

Getting THE Call for Job Interviews and Offers

Then, I asked John if he could defend these transferrable skills and achievements with either some form of documentation (diploma, certificate, transcripts, and past performance reviews), or a great PAR story to tell to convince them, or a personal reference from his past that can confirm his skills.

With this information, I prepared to write his Selected Achievements and Skills, Level 6 adding his transferrable skills and key words.

Selected Achievements and Skills

Managed the successful completion of a $250,000, one-month, detailed, motorized shade installation project for the Ransom County, Taylor Museum of Contemporary Art. As a subcontractor with JE Dunn, coordinated with numerous stakeholders including museum owners, electricians, architects, and other subcontractors, completed the project ahead of schedule, under budget, with outstanding client reviews.

Led the efforts of 95 associates, as the Assistant Store Manager, for a $2.4 Million per month Albertson's Food Store in Sacramento, CA. Inspired team cohesion, improving performance and moral. Trained and mentored team members to enhance their professional development and improve customer service.

Supervised and conducted on-site inspections to monitor compliance which consistently saved money by getting the job done right the first time and eliminating costly rework. Streamlined procedures and operations to achieve more in the same amount of time.

<u>Skills:</u> Strong written and verbal communication skills. Personable and capable of working with all levels of management and technical leads. Proficient in problem solving, implementing complex solutions, scale drawings, contracts, obtaining bids and administering complex projects. Results and customer focused. International travel includes Korea, Malaysia, and Singapore.

<u>Note:</u> I added more key words and transferrable skills above.

Suggestions to develop your achievements:

Start each achievement with an action verb in the past tense (managed, led, and supervised). After the verb, tell your quantifiable results (with numbers!), include PCF/BOE related information, and include the details (PAR stories) that show how difficult it was to complete.

LEVEL 7: CAREER OVERVIEW

The final level is a very important level even though it appears to be just a work history. It serves a valuable purpose; to diminish your liabilities. With a chronological resume, it's much easier to find flaws in your resume. The last ten years is what the employer needs to see. Going back more than 10 years may make you look too old.

This format diminishes the adverse effects of several liabilities.

It doesn't highlight liabilities like age, lack of career progression, most of your work experience in only one industry, or gaps in work. The content that precedes this level is so strong that any adverse effects are minimized. You're still providing the same information, but in a way to highlight your assets and diminish your liabilities.

Career Overview

    Alabama University – Graduate Student, 2007-2011

    John's Home Improvement Company, AL – Owner, 2004-Present

    Schmidt Construction, WA – Construction Superintendent, 2002-2004

    Albertson's Food Stores, CA - Assistant Store Manager, 1994-2002

Getting THE Call for Job Interviews and Offers

WHAT DOES A COMPELLING RESUME LOOK LIKE?

John Brown

1111 Windsor Drive, Summit Mills, AL 68654; 913.123.9876; jbrown@gmail.com

Design and Build Architect

Project / Project Manager / Plan / Design / Coordinate / Estimate Costs / Administer / Construction / Architecture / Architect / Engineer / Scale Drawings / Contracts / Client Review / Obtain Bid / Award Contract / Monitor Compliance / On-site Observation / CAD / Prepare Drawings / Zoning / Building Code

Career professional with a Master's degree in Architecture plus sixteen years of experience working with Albertson's, JE Dunn, Turner Construction, Walton, Raul Construction and as a business owner and entrepreneur. Key leadership roles in Food Store Management and the Residential and Commercial Construction industries.

Career Track: Professional growth as Assistant Store Manager, Construction Superintendent, Entrepreneur, and Home Improvement Business Owner.

Utilized principle centered leadership in managing multiple projects consisting of technical teams and subcontractors and developing partnerships and programs. Strong track record of increased responsibility, planning, designing, streamlining business processes, with excellent "word-of-mouth" customer satisfaction. Demonstrated entrepreneurial spirit that increased sales and profits.

Proven Record: Skilled at negotiating, estimating, budgeting, scheduling, monitoring compliance, on-site inspections, contracts, and conflict resolution. Consistently exceeded company standards for quality of work and completed requirements on-time, under budget, with excellent client reviews. Completed both a Bachelor's and Master's degree in Architecture at Alabama University concurrent with running his own home improvement business as an entrepreneur, taking 18-21 credit hours per semester.

Education and Special Training:

Bachelor and Master's Degrees in Architecture from Alabama University, School of Architecture

Computer: Drafting (AutoCAD), Modeling (SketchUp, Revit), Graphics (Photoshop, Illustrator, Indesign), MS Office (Word, Outlook, Excel, and PowerPoint)

Construction: Carpentry (rough and finish), tile work, paint finishes, interior shading systems and floor plans for both spec and custom homes. Knowledgeable of building codes for AL, WA, and CA

Selected Achievements and Skills:

- Managed the successfully completion of a $250,000, one-month, detailed, motorized shade installation project for the Ransom County, Taylor Museum of Contemporary Art. As a subcontractor with JE Dunn, coordinated with numerous stakeholders including museum owners, electricians, architects, and other subcontractors, completed the project ahead of schedule, under budget, with outstanding client reviews.
- Led the efforts of 95 associates, as the Assistant Store Manager, for a $2.4 Million per month Albertson's Food Store in Sacramento, CA. Inspired team cohesion, improving performance and moral. Trained and mentored team members to enhance their professional development and improve customer service.
- Supervised and conducted on-site inspections to monitor compliance which consistently saved money by getting the job done right the first time and eliminating costly rework. Streamlined procedures and operations to achieve more in the same amount of time.

Skills: Strong written and verbal communication skills. Personable and capable of working with all levels of management and technical leads. Proficient in problem solving, implementing complex solutions, scale drawings, contracts, obtaining bids and administering complex projects. Results and customer focused. International travel includes Korea, Malaysia, and Singapore.

Career Overview:

Alabama University – Graduate Student, 2007-2011
John's Home Improvement Company, AL – Owner, 2004-Present
Schmidt Construction, WA – Construction Superintendent, 2002-2004
Albertson's Food Stores, CA – Assistant Store Manager, 1994-2002

Did this process strengthen your resume?

If you did STEPS 1-3, from Chapter 5, to the best of your ability, you should have two pages worth of details that will make a major difference to your resume and whether you receive a phone call. If not, go back and do it again – until you do. Use the same process to create your own Best Compelling Resume from top to bottom. Just make sure it speaks PCF/BOE.

HOW DO YOU BUILD YOUR SPECIAL PURPOSE RESUMES?

Now that you've finished your Best Compelling Resume, there are still a few things left to do:

- First, don't forget to do a final spell check of your resume. Your computer will tell you that you have sentence fragments – that's okay! Just make sure everything is spelled correctly. Remember to delete all articles (a, an & the).

- Second, have someone proof read your resume to ensure it makes sense and all jargon, acronyms and abbreviations are defined the first time they appear.

- Third, check your resume for any exaggerations, opinions, and superlatives, that can't be supported. This could cause you not to get a phone call. So, be careful! Just state the facts (not your opinion) and let the interviewer decide how good you are.

- Finally, it's time to convert your Compelling Resume into three Special Purpose Resumes; a Face-to-face Networking Resume (to hand-carry, hardcopy), an Advertised Job Resume (only used to apply for advertised positions found in the paper or on the web), and a Web Resume (for Job Banks and Social Networking Sites).

Face-to-Face Networking Resume

Your Face-to-Face Networking Resume, a paper/hardcopy version, is the same as the Compelling Resume except that the Level 3 (key words) section is deleted because it's not needed. However, it is no more than one page in length. This resume is designed to be hand delivered to others at advice meetings, visits, when meeting someone for lunch, Job Fairs, and any other opportunity to network.

Advertised Job Resume

This version of your resume is used when applying for advertised positions that you find in the newspaper, trade magazines, or on the web. This resume is the same as your Compelling Resume except that the Level 2 (position titles) is deleted, because they don't apply.

Web Resume

Anytime you post your resume on the web (Job Banks, Social Networking Sites, Monster.com, CareerBuilder.com, etc.), convert your Compelling Resume into a Plain Text document. The length here is not an issue. Some sites accept Word docs; however, many won't recognize specialized text, bullets, tabs, boldface or formatted text. Your resumes, unless converted, run the risk of showing up on an interviewer's computer screen as gibberish. You can avoid formatting issues by saving it as a Text Only/Plain Text document.

After you've saved it, open your resume and this is what you should see:

John Brown

111 Wind Drive, Summit Mills, AL 68654; 913.123.9876; jbrown@gmail.com

Design and Build Architect

Project / Project Manager / Plan / Design / Coordinate / Estimate Costs / Administer / Construction / Architecture / Architect / Engineer / Scale Drawings / Contract Documents / Client Review / Obtain Bid / Award Contract / Monitor Compliance / On-site Observation / CAD / Prepare Report / Zoning / Building Code

Now, separate the major sections of your resume with the space bar and capitalize the major headings and resave it in Text Only/Plain Text document.

Discover the Job Searching SECRETS Employer's Don't Want You to Know.

This is what you should see;

JOHN BROWN

111 Wind Drive, Summit Mills, AL 68654

913.123.9876

jbrown@gmail.com

DESIGN AND BUILD ARCHITECT

Project / Project Manager / Plan / Design / Coordinate / Estimate Costs / Administer / Construction / Architecture / Architect / Engineer / Scale Drawings / Contract Documents / Client Review / Obtain Bid / Award Contract / Monitor Compliance / On-site Observation / CAD / Prepare Report / Zoning / Building Code

---

Notice how re-spacing and capitalizing makes your resume more readable. Once posted, again re-space and capitalize so it's readable. When finished, email it to yourself - so you can see what it looks like.

Then, go back and make any final edits to ensure it looks the way you want it to look on the web site.

Now you have a resume you can post on Facebook in the About me box, and on LinkedIn.com. These special purpose resumes have produced considerably more phone calls for my clients because now the employer can clearly see the skills, talents, and abilities they can contribute to their PCF/BOE related achievements.

Did this help you strengthen your resume? Do you now have a better understanding of how to write and speak in the language every employer understands?

CHAPTER 7:
19+ PROVEN WAYS TO GET THE INTERVIEW

"One important key to success is self-confidence. An important key to self-confidence is preparation." –Arthur Ashe

Since you know how to create your Best Master Resume and your three specialty resumes (for advertised job, web, and face-to-face networking), you're ready to get them in front of the right people.

First, let's define the term, the right people. The right people are those folks who make the hiring decisions; the leaders within a company. Right now, you don't have a clue who these people are, and they don't know you exist. That's okay because you don't need to know that right now. You'll discover that later.

Let's take a closer look at the 19+ proven ways of getting your resume in front of the right people to get the call for job interviews and offers.

1: Use Major Job Sites

monster.com	thejobplanet.com
careerbuilder.com	myjobhunter.com
indeed.com	linkedin.com/jobs
hotjobs.yahoo.com	usa.gov or usajobs.gov
dice.com	
usajobs.com	theladders.com
jobcentral.com	jobs.net
jobankinfo.com	Google+
simplyhired.com	findtherightjob.com

Job.com and Craigslist.com: Great resource for local jobs, career advice, and other services to help you manage your career and job.

Executive Search Online: Leading nationwide job matching service for more experienced executives.

Beyond.com: Extensive career network that's set up as a community of niche sites in various industries.

Snagajob.com: Online tool to help you find hourly jobs. This service provides you with access to part-time and full-time hourly jobs.

GoFreelance.com: Community for freelance professionals and companies looking to hire skilled freelance experts for thousands of freelance and work-at-home jobs in the US and worldwide.

ResumeRabbit.com: Get all the benefits without all the work. Fill out one simple form, and you're instantly posted on over 80 job boards like CareerBuilder, Job.com, Net-Temps, and Dice. It takes ten minutes to complete and saves 60 hours of research and data entry.

Repost your resume every 30 days because most employers and recruiters will only search resumes that have been posted in the last 30 days.

Use a Job Search Agent:

A Job Search Agent is a specialized search that you can set up on many job posting sites. Specify the types of jobs you're looking for, and the job search agent notifies you by email whenever a new job that meets your criteria is posted. This is an invaluable tool in your job search. Set up a job search agents on all major job posting sites.

2: Use Recruiter Sites

Search the web for recruiters who handle your industry, professional specialty, or function. Ensure they have your updated resume and any specifics concerning restrictions or constraints to your placement. If you are doing an industry or functional change, recruiters will not be of much help. Recruiters are looking for people who have extensive experience (5+ years) in a specific industry or function. No follow up is required here. For example: recruitersonline.com, therecruiternetwork.com, and ziprecruiter.com.

Use Resume Mailman:

If you don't know any recruiters and would like to have your resume sent to recruiters that specialize in your industry, they will email your resume to targeted recruiters.

3: Use Temporary Employment Sites

Temporary employment/staffing agencies offer several advantages. They can get you inside-the-castle to meet people in companies on your *Target List* - where you would otherwise not have access. They also get a finder's fee if you become a permanent hire. Many smart employers find their best permanent employees after trying them as temps. For example: Manpower, Kelly, ADECCO, and yellowpages.com.

4: Use Social Networking Sites

50% of employers admit visiting these sites before making a final hiring decision.

According to *Dan Schawbel*, author of *Me 2.0*, the Top 10 Social Networking Sites for finding jobs are:

LinkedIn.com: Optimize your profile, cultivate your network, join, and participate in groups, use applications, and exchange endorsements. Use a distinct URL like; LinkedIn.com/in/yourfullname and a picture that best represents you. When searching, recognize who in your network might be able to help you get to the hiring manager. You're given 1st, 2nd and 3rd-degree connections that you can use to secure a job opportunity.

Plaxo: Create your profile with a section about you, your contact info, and your pulse stream (which is made up of your presence on social media sites like Twitter). You're even able to share your photo album and send eCards. Plaxo has an address book that keeps track of all your contact info and integrates with Simply Hired, which searches thousands of job sites and aggregates them in a single location. After building your profile, use it for jobs on Simply Hired.

Twitter: Twitter breaks down barriers and lets you talk directly to hiring managers, without having to submit a resume. Even though it's probably one of the best networking tools, it needs to be linked to a blog or LinkedIn.com profile. You can't hire someone based on a Twitter profile, without having a link to something that gives more info. You get to add one URL to your profile.

Jobster: Jobster is a powerful platform for networking with employers who are offering jobs, while you're searching. You can upload your resume, embed your video resume, showcase links to your site, your picture, and tag your skills. You can search for open positions and see who the person is that posted the job. Then you can add them to your network and connect with them to find out more about the position.

Facebook: You'll be able to see who listed the ad and then message them to show interest. When you find a job opening you're interested in, message the hiring manager directly. Also, join groups and fan pages to find people with common interests and network with them.

Getting THE Call for Job Interviews and Offers

Craigslist: Most positions are for consultants (design/programming help) at small to midsize companies. There are new listings every day, and if you wake up to this site every morning and refresh the page, you have a good chance at getting a job sooner rather than later.

MyWorkster: It focuses on exclusive networks for colleges, allowing students and alumni to connect for exclusive career opportunities. It allows you to create a profile and network with employers. For free, you get a profile, instant messenger built in the site, groups, events, your resume and more. It uses Facebook Connect to get your info.

VisualCV: Instead of a traditional resume, you get your own branded webpage, to add video, audio, images, graphs, charts, work samples, presentations, and references. It lets you stand out by communicating your value in a way that's not possible with static text. You can display it publicly or privately, email it to a recruiter, save it as a PDF or forward the URL, which will rank high for your name.

Ecademy: You have your online profile, where you can tell people what you do. You can join business networking groups based on your expertise and exchange messages with other members privately. You can also ask for introductions from friends from LinkedIn.com.

JobFox: It tries to pair you with a job that best fits you. Their Mutual Suitability SystemTM enables them to match your wants to those of employers to find the best relationship. The system learns about your skills, experiences, and goals and then presents you with jobs. Then there's the Jobfox Intro, where both the applicant and company get emails to encourage the connection. Like VisualCV, you get your own branded website, with a personal web address to send to employers.

Note: Social networking will consume a lot of time and should *only* be done before 9 AM and after 4 PM? From 9 AM to 4 PM, you are either on the phone or face-to-face with people who can help you. Continue to use the other 18+ Proven ways to get your resume in front of the right people to make your phone ring for job interviews and offers.

Remember: Anyone trying to help you needs three things; what you want to do (titles of positions), what companies you'd love to work for (your Target List), and your resume.

Caution: Make sure you revisit all social networking sites that you're already on and remove any objectionable material including anything of a sexual, bad humor, racial, political, or religious nature.

5: Contact People I Know (PIK)

The people you know and the people they know (referrals) provide your best opportunity for finding your next position.

65% of jobs in America are filled by networking with people they already know.

If you're a business owner, when you need good people, who and where are you going to go to first. How about family, friends, neighbors, coworkers, colleagues, venders, and suppliers? Armed with this knowledge, let's see how this can help you.

Contact everyone on your PIK list.

Make a list of everyone you know. This list will become your contact list because you're now going to communicate to them (via USPS, LinkedIn.com or Facebook) and ask for their help.

You're communicating with them because they need to know three things; what you want to do (titles of positions you're seeking), your *Target List* of companies you'd love to work for, and a copy of your resume.

If you're connected with them on LinkedIn.com or Facebook, this information should be accessible to them on the site. If not, just send them a letter USPS (or email). Use whatever works best – just as long as they get the three items listed above. You're going to ask everyone you know for referrals from people that they know who work in your targeted companies.

Who you know is less important than who they know.

Don't prejudge anyone!

Excluding someone, just because you think they wouldn't know anyone important, is a mistake.

For example: In 1996, I lived in Seattle. One of my clients had Microsoft on their Target List. My client's wife had a brother, John, who worked for a pool cleaning company. One of his clients was the Gates family (CEO of Microsoft at the time) and was on a first name basis with the entire family.

John mentioned that his brother-in-law wanted to work at Microsoft. Long story short, a month later, my client was working there. How powerful is that?

So, get serious and don't leave anyone out. *Pull-Out-All-the-Stops.* Get your fear and pride out of your way. Who do you know? Who does your spouse know? Who do your kids know?

Keep contacting everyone that you know and everyone your family members know.

Sample PIK Letter (Hardcopy-USPS):

I hope all is well with you, Susan, and the kids.

I'm writing this letter to ask for your help. I'm looking for a new position as VP/Director of Human Resources in the Telecom industry here in Kansas City.

If you know of anyone who could use my talents and abilities, please give my resume to that person.

Also, I've targeted the following companies that I would love to work for: (add from your Target List).

My goal is to speak with people who work for these companies. My biggest obstacle right now is that I don't know anyone who works for them. If you, or any of your friends or associates, know of anyone in these target companies that I could speak with, I would appreciate the referral.

I have no intention of asking them for a position, nor do I expect that they would know of any job openings. I only wish to speak with them about how my background and experience relates to their industry within the local area.

Attached is my resume for your review. I'd like to call you in the next few days to follow up on this letter.

Thank you in advance for anything you can do to help in my search.

Note: This letter is for people you're not yet connected to via Facebook or LinkedIn.com. For those you're already connected with on the web, just modify the above letter and add it to your communications to them on the web.

6: Send Approach Letters

You've already created a *Target List* of the 10-15 companies you would like to work for (part of your *Focus Statement*) (or are closest to your home). It's now time to send *Approach* (#6), and *Advice* Letters (#7) to your Target Companies. *Approach Letters* are sent to the company Leaders (without a referral), and *Advice Letters* are sent to Target Companies where you have a referral from the people you know - asking for an advice meeting.

In 1995, while living in Kansas and moving to Seattle, I sent an approach letter to 7 target companies in Seattle. A month later, I ended up working for one of them.

An *Approach Letter* is a letter you mail (USPS) to each company on your Target List. Mail it to the company Leadership, 2 to 3 levels above the position you want.

Sample Approach Letter (no resume attached):

If building long-term, international marketing relationships and increasing your competitive advantage in the marketplace appeals to you, then I can get the job done!

As a dedicated international senior business executive with over 20+ years of progressively responsible management experience within the global sales arena, I have managed high-tech sales, marketing, operations, and product management in all major world market regions (Europe, Middle East, Asia, and Latin America).

Additionally, I have directed overseas product introduction, trade shows, and key account supervision and distributor management. My strengths and achievements include:

> *List a few strong achievements here as bullet points. Make it PCF/BOE rich!*

Of course, there is a great deal more to my background. While I am not sure of your staffing needs for the near future, I would appreciate the opportunity to meet with you to discuss how my talents could contribute to meeting your needs.

I will call you soon to arrange a brief office call at a mutually convenient time to discuss how I can add value to your organization. I look forward to meeting you.

7: Send Advice Letters

As you contact your *People I Know* (PIK) and receive referrals from people who already work in your Target Companies, send this person (the referral) an *Advice Letter* requesting an Advice Meeting.

Purpose: To gain information and to be favorably remembered.

An *Advice Meeting* is a brief 15-minute meeting designed to ask for advice as to how your background and experience relate to their industry. During the meeting, ask relevant questions about their industry, your resume and what's missing that would make you more competitive in their industry. At the end of the meeting, request a referral to others that could also provide advice. Since they now know who you are and what you can do, the potential exists to be called, if a future need arises.

Sample Advice Letter (with a referral):

Your name was referred to me by a mutual friend; Bill Reynolds. He indicated that you would be the ideal person to speak with to offer some advice as to how I should proceed with my career.

The purpose of my letter is to ask your advice as to how my background and experience relate to your industry.

I have no intention of asking you for a position, nor do I expect that you would know of an opening. My only purpose is to ask for your candid advice as to how my background and experience relates to your industry.

My resume is attached for your review and comment. I will call you next week to set a time for us to meet.

Approach Letters are sent to the company Leaders (without a referral), and *Advice Letters* are sent to referrals from the people you know - asking for an advice meeting. Both letters are sent to companies on your Target List.

Why do some letters go without a resume?

In most cases, the person you're sending the letter to is not the person who opens the letter. And, when the letter is opened by someone else, they are often told to either throw letters away that have resumes attached or to send them to Human Resources. My experience is that your letter has a much better chance of being read by the addressee if the resume is not attached. Instead, add your best achievements in the body of your letter.

8: Visit Your Target Companies

Here's what I did while living in Seattle. Years ago, I got laid-off due to a lack of positive cash flow in my company. I did a web search for all similar type companies in the Seattle area, and I found three. I called the first company and spoke with the receptionist and said,

> *My name is _____, and I'm very interested in your company. Is there anyone there I can speak with concerning what it takes to join your team?*

She told me that I was in luck. That very afternoon, their company president was flying in to address several investors to their business at 2 PM. After I thanked her, I put on my suit and tie, drove to their office, and sat in their conference room to listen to the Presidents business plan.

After the briefing, I walked up to the President, stuck out my hand, and said,

> *I enjoyed your presentation. My name is _____. I just have one question. What does it take for me to join your team?*

He then asked me what I did. I gave him my 30-second commercial. He asked me for my resume and said someone would contact me. Then, he left hurriedly because he had another engagement.

The next day, I was invited back to meet with the Branch Manager. I was asked to make a brief presentation the next day and was hired the following day.

I admit I did have the credentials and experience. But, I also know this technique works because good employers are always looking for the best talent they can find to help them enhance their PCF/SOE.

Getting THE Call for Job Interviews and Offers

Here's my challenge to you:
Go visit every company on your target list. 90% of success in life is showing up, asking questions, and showing an interest.

Purpose: To confirm or deny your interest in the company.

That's right. Show up (unannounced) at each company on your *Target List* and strike up a conversation.

> *Hi, my name is _____, and I'm very interested in your company. Is there anyone here that I could speak with to find out what it takes to join your team?*

You'll probably be directed to either the Boss or someone from personnel or human resources. When you meet them, say the same thing. If anyone asks what you do – give them your 30-Second Commercial and your face-to-face networking resume.

Stay awhile to chat with them, but not too long. Show a genuine interest in their company. Impress them with your knowledge of their company because of your research.

Be prepared to go right to a job interview, if they have the time or set a time to come back. Be prepared to present your resume and your achievements.

Note: For more on interviewing strong enough to receive a job offer, please see *Interview Like You Mean It:* How to interview strong enough to receive a job offer.

Also, be prepared in the case they say, *we're not hiring right now.* That's just an excuse from someone who's not responsible for the company's Profit and Loss. In response to this statement just say,

> *Thank you for that information. May I speak with the head of your Engineering Department (or whatever functional department you are interested in) just to ask a few questions?*

If you are turned down again, ask,

> *Maybe I could just write him. Could you please give me his name?*

Be nice and respectful, but assertive. Take note of what you learned and follow up later.

I love this quote from *Hannibal:* *"We will either find a way or make one."*

By showing up unannounced at your target companies, you're creating opportunities that previously didn't exist! Think about it!

9: Send Emerging Opportunity Letters

Emerging opportunities happen all the time. Look for opportunities in the business section of the local newspaper. Look for announcements of promotions, new people coming in to Lead departments or divisions. Write these people an Emerging Opportunity letter and follow up to see what you can do to help them.

Sample Emerging Opportunity Letter (no resume attached):

> *I noticed the announcement of your promotion in the Business Section of the Kansas City Star Newspaper this past Sunday as the new Chief Operations Officer for Sprint. Congratulations!*
>
> *I just wanted to take the opportunity to introduce myself. Much of my background has been directly related to Operations within the Telecom industry. A few of my achievements include;*
>
> - *Quadrupled revenue, as VP of Operations, from $5 Million to $20 Million in 18 months*
> - *Directed strategy, as Director of Operations, that increased profits by $10 Million, annually*
>
> *I will contact you soon to discuss what I can do to add value to your team.*

Format your resume for email:

When emailing a resume, you have 2-options; either insert the resume in the body of the email or as an attachment. Review the job posting to see if there is a preferred method. Formatting is also crucial. Plain text (.txt) files are a safe bet, but Microsoft Word documents (.doc) and PDFs (.pdf) are often accepted and allow you greater control over layout and design.

If you send a resume as an attachment, save it first as MS Word 97 – 2003 formatted document (.doc). This way anyone can open your resume. If you send it in MS Word 2010, only people that have Windows 7 (.docx) can open the file.

10: Contact College Classmates and Alumni

Sample email (or letter) to classmates and fellow alumni:

> *I need your help! I'm a graduate of the Class of XXXX, and I'm seeking the following position;*
>
> *(List titles, function, industry, compensation, and location you're your Focus Statement).*
>
> *If you know of anyone who could use my skills, please provide my resume to that person.*
>
> *Thank you in advance for any help you might be able to provide. I've attached my resume for your review.*

Ensure to follow up to these emails/letters (especially if you know the person). Also, ask your Alma Mater for their help in finding you a new position (most have a Career Placement Office to assist their graduates to find work), and a list of all graduates who live in the geographic area where you intend to work.

WHAT ARE THE TOP 5 PROVEN METHODS USING SOCIAL EVENTS?

The following events happen all the time and are great opportunities to present your *30-Second Commercial*, present your Face-to-Face Networking Resume, set up future advice meetings, and exchange business cards.

They offer the greatest opportunity to meet people who're also working in your chosen industry or functional area.

11: Attend all conventions, seminars, or workshops are excellent opportunities to meet people.

12: Get involved with all chapters of applicable associations, societies, and clubs that have anything to do with your field or function (including hobbies) are great ways to meet new people. Find out when the next meeting is scheduled and make sure you attend.

13: Attend all monthly/quarterly Chamber of Commerce meetings/events (in your town and adjacent towns).

14: Attend all Social Events (like parties, traveling, athletic events, weddings, reunions, barbecues, and holiday gatherings) are great opportunities to network.

15: Attend all Job Fairs. Dress for an interview. Prescreen each booth as to what positions they're trying to fill. If they're not looking for someone with your Focus, go to the next booth. If they're looking for people with your Focus, give them your resume. Also, record their name, company, and phone number (business card) – so you can call them a day or two after the event to continue the conversation.

To be successful, attack the job market by making someone else's phone ring, instead of sitting home and waiting for your phone to ring.

Give networking cards to all you meet:

A networking card is the professional way of getting your name out. Having to write your name and phone number on a napkin is not an impressive way to start a business relationship. If you don't have a card, have a few hundred prepared that list your name, phone number, email, and your desired title, function, or work specialty from your Focus. This will make it easier for them to remember you when you reconnect. I use *Vistaprint.com*.

Sample Networking Card:

JOHN BROWN

"Design and Build Architect"

101 NE Tally Road
Summit Mills, MO 64321
816.123.8821
john.brown@kc.rr.com

"If it is to be, it is up to me"

Also, ask for their card as well. If they don't have a card, just write their name and number on the back of one of your cards. When you receive a business card, take the time to write the date and location on the back - to help you remember them later.

According to *Jeff Snyder, securityrecruiter.com*, you can add a *Quick Response (or QR) code* to your card, to be scanned by a smartphone and linked to either your WordPress Blog or your LinkedIn.com page.

16: Contact Family Members and Close Friends

A career search is one of the hardest things you'll ever do. If your friends and family don't know what you're trying to do, and they're not given the opportunity to help, your search will be much harder and take considerably longer.

The worst thing you could ever do when you've lost your job is to keep your search a secret.

Get your Pride and Fear out of the way and ask for help! The most important commodity you have is your attitude. And, having someone to talk to will make all the difference. Make sure they have your resume, *Target List,* and *Focus Statement.*

Friends

It is my joy in life to find
At every turning of the road
The strong arms of a comrade kind
To help me onward with my load;
And since I have no gold to give
And love alone must make amends,
My only prayer is, while I live -
God make me worthy of my friends.

- Anonymous

Here's the most powerful job finding technique!

17: Find a Personal Sponsor

This technique is especially powerful with good friends and/or family members who know you well. Sponsors are those who agree to do two things:

> ***First***, to hand-carry your resume to both the Senior Human Resources person in their company and the Senior Hiring Manager for the position you're seeking
>
> ***Second***, to offer a strong positive verbal recommendation

When I've seen this happen, it normally produced an interview.

18: Let's Do Lunch

This technique was developed by one of my clients that helped him find his position and here's his testimonial:

> *"Good news Ed! Since our last contact, I have accepted the position of CFO, and I feel that our work together was a successful joint venture and I sincerely appreciated your personal concern, encouragement, and guidance."* - Thomas A., Seattle, WA

Tom essentially took someone to lunch several times a week. He would either invite someone he knew (a PIK) or someone he was referred to by a PIK (a Referral). The lunch meeting eventually turned into an advice meeting. Tom would explain his situation and ask for advice as to how his background and experience related to their industry/business.

Tom would end the meeting by asking for a referral, providing a copy of his resume, and following up later to offer assistance and to maintain the relationship.

One of the most important lesson's I've learned about building lasting relationships quickly is to invite the other person to share a meal with you. If you want to get to know someone, there's something magic about *breaking bread* with them.

Breaking Bread together is the secret to building lasting relationships. It turns acquaintances into friends and friends into good friends.

Remember: Networking is 80% what you can do for others and 20% what they can do for you. So, get out there and serve others (volunteer, get involved, do something for them, lift others) and networking will take care of itself.

19: Apply for Advertised Positions

Raise your aim when applying for advertised positions. You'll find these positions in industry related magazines, newspapers and on the Internet. Only apply if you meet 90% of their requirements,

Don't lower your point of aim by applying for positions for which you're overqualified.

This is what most people do. Ads are designed to fill less than 15% of the low-medium paying jobs. This is only one way of getting the call for job interviews and offers.

For example: If you have a college degree and you apply for a position that does not require a college degree, you're wasting your time - because you're overqualified.

This is the Secret - because most people apply for every job they know they can do or would like to do. Later, they complain because they never got a response, which only adds to their frustration.

And, here are two additional Proven Ways:

> **Proven Way 20:** When you read the *specific* job description, if you notice things that you have done before or other qualifications that you have, that are *not* in your resume, add them before you respond to the advertised job.
>
> **Proven Way 21:** If you apply for a great job, add the company to your Target List, ask your network if they know of anyone who works in that company, send advice and approach letters, visit the company, and do all you can do to create opportunities that previously didn't exist.

Getting THE Call for Job Interviews and Offers

The best use of your resume is as a leave – behind document, not to precede you. Get out there and use all the proven ways from this book.

Using Cover Letters:

My experience tells me that your resume is what generates the call for an interview – not a cover letter. If a cover letter is required, which is *rare*, here's a simple format to use;

<u>Sample Cover Letter Format:</u>

To Whom It May Concern: (If no name is available)

The purpose of my letter is to apply for the position of ...

Accordingly, I have attached my resume for your review.

In the job description, you are seeking someone who has.......

   Here are my qualifications;

   Add a few bullet points (achievements) from your resume

I look forward to the opportunity of speaking with you further about what I can do for your company.

How many of these proven ways have you used so far? What's holding you back?

Discover the Job Searching SECRETS Employer's Don't Want You to Know.

CHAPTER 8:
INTERVIEWING TO RECEIVE THE JOB OFFER

"A winning effort begins with preparation."
-Joe Gibbs

Interviewing is a game! And your mission, if you accept, is to win. How do you do that?

- Be likable, relax, and have fun
- Focus your PAR stories on their job description
- Show desire, interest, and enthusiasm
- Follow up!
- Practice, Practice, Practice – via Role-Play

If you do these simple things, you'll make the interviewer's job much easier and you'll be given the offer.

Understand the Purpose of Job Interviews

What's the primary purpose of an interview? Most people think the purpose is to find the best person for the job. However, this is false. The true purpose of any interview is to de-select, screen-out everyone, so there's just one person left (or a short list). How can you avoid being screened-out?

Understand the questions the employer will be silently asking about you:

- **Can he do the job and do it well (competence)?**
- **Will he fit in with us (likability, social skills)?**
- **Can we afford him (compensation)?**
- **Does he really want to be one of us or just want a job (enthusiasm)?**

If, during the interview, they get a *No* or *I'm not sure* to any of the above questions, the interview is over; they just forgot to tell you. Your job, if you decide to accept, is to *not* get screened out! So, how do you do that? Keep reading!

Select your professional references carefully:

This is an important choice.

> *Whomever you select as a reference could either seal or sink your chances of being selected.*

Caution: Carefully choose 3-5 people to act as a reference for you. Select those who you've worked with in the last 3-5 years who can comment positively on your work ethic and integrity. Include some supervisors, peers, and subordinates for best results. Ensure you ask their permission before putting them on your reference list (so they are expecting the call) and provide them with a copy of your resume. You'll be glad you did because they'll have it available when talking to potential employers.

What's a PAR Story?

A good PAR story includes these three components:

    Problem: What problem or situation did you encounter?

    Action: What action did you take to deal with the situation?

    Result: What was the result of your action?

The key to a good PAR story is to select a problem, like what the employer is expecting, that has a decisive action, and a stellar result.

For example:

> *In May of 20XX, I was faced with this challenge…*
>
> *I decided to…*
>
> *A month later the situation stabilized and we avoided a ….*

Craft your PAR stories carefully. They should show how the magnitude and seriousness of the situation you faced, tell the decisive and immediate actions you took, and conclude with the stellar and quantifiable results that followed.

Did you make a difference for your former employers? Did you make things better than you found them? Tell us the story in PAR format and tell it convincingly!

Your PAR stories are what creates and reinforces your *Perceived Value Added*. The strong you *Perceive Value Added*, the more *Leverage* you have.

A good Request, has three components:

- <u>Topic</u>: Concerning the starting salary….
- <u>Justification</u>: Based on my having an MBA….
- <u>Question</u>: Let me ask this, is that possible? Or, is there anything else you can do?

<u>Important</u>: Every time you ask for something, you need to justify your request. If you have a good reason, your chances are good that your request will be approved.

Prepare for a Phone Screening Interview

Before you'll be scheduled for a face-to-face interview, you will receive a phone call, which is your screening interview. If you pass the screening interview, you'll be invited to visit.

Be prepared to receive a phone interview. When you're on the phone in an interview – stand up! This will make you sound better. Also, if you can be in front of a mirror, smile as you speak. This will help with your tonality - how they perceive your level of interest.

Have their job description in front of you and tell your PAR stories related to the transferrable skills found in their job description. Focus on their job description and avoid any distractions around you.

So, you don't waste your time (or theirs) interviewing for a position you would never accept, pre-screen the caller by asking a few questions.

Screen the Screener!

Sample Screening Questions:

- Any travel involved and is this a contract or a full-time position?
- What does the position require? What's the job description?
- Any sales involved? If you don't want sales, tell them.
- Where is the office located? (some positions are in other cities and/or states)
- Does this position require me to supervise others? How many? Who?
- What's the range for compensation? If you need $70,000 and they say $35,000, be honest and decline.
- What benefits come with this position? If you need medical benefits this job does not include it – decline.

In fact, if you don't like their answers, politely *decline* their request for interview. Don't lead them on. Make the decision early concerning what you'll accept and what you'll decline.

- If they're an employer or a company recruiter, don't answer questions about pay, other than to say, *I'm very open, flexible and compensation's negotiable.*
- If they're from a recruiting company, or an independent recruiter, answer all their questions honestly (tell him your pay range).

Getting THE Call for Job Interviews and Offers

WHAT DO YOU DO BEFORE THE INTERVIEW?

Focus on their Specific Job Description:

Your focus during any interview is on their specific job description from the job ad. All the people interviewing you will be grading you on your ability to do the job. The only way they can answer this question is to compare you to their job description. The closer the match – the stronger you are as a candidate. So, just replicate the same transferrable skills that are found in their job description in your PAR stories. For example: If the job description specifies that the job is a planning job and all your PAR stories involve your ability to design, they won't see you as good match. If you want to make the job easier for the interviewer, make your PAR Stories match the transferrable skills listed in the specific job description.

Sample Specific Job Description:

Let's assume this is a specific job description (below) from the job ad for which you are being interviewed. What transferrable skills are they seeking? They're bolded. What buzz-words should you add to your PAR stories? They're underlined.

> *Plans layout of project and integrates engineering elements into unified design for client review and approval. Prepares scale drawings and contract documents for building contractors. Represents client in obtaining bids and awarding construction contracts. Administers construction contracts and conducts periodic on-site observation of work during construction to monitor compliance with plans. May prepare operating and maintenance manuals, studies, and reports. May use computer-assisted design software and equipment to prepare project designs and plans.*

Which transferrable skills will you prepare PAR stories for use during the interview?

> *Plan, integrate, prepare, design, represent, obtain, award, administer, conduct, integrate, monitor, and direct*

Have you ever demonstrated these transferable skills before? Do you own these skills? If so, prepare and practice your PAR stories.

It's that easy! Don't mess it up!

Show up 15-minutes early!

It may seem obvious, but if you're not on time for your interview, this could get you screened out. Getting there early makes a good impression on the interviewer and allows you to take a few deep breaths, organize your thoughts, refresh your memory on any points that you've found difficult in your practice interviews and scan any company materials that may be available in the waiting room. It also allows you to use the restroom, if needed. Freshen your breath and make any last-minute checks and adjustments.

Arriving early is easiest when you've planned your route. Whatever your mode of transportation, make sure you have directions to your destination, along with a back-up route, in case an unexpected delay.

Have the phone number of the interviewer or receptionist to notify in case you're running late.

It's also highly recommended that you perform a dry run a few days before your interview. Travel to the interview location and be sure you know how to get there and where to park without getting lost or delayed.

Getting THE Call for Job Interviews and Offers

WHAT SHOULD YOU ASK DURING THE INTERVIEW?

You'll be judged on the quality of the questions you ask! If you don't ask questions, it could be perceived as a lack of preparation or interest. Ask good questions! Do your homework!

Employers like candidates who know what they want from a job. They're also impressed with someone who's done some research before the interview. Make the effort to research the organization you're interested in, and you'll be ahead of your competition.

Your job is to interview them to see if this job is a good match for you. If it's not a good match, don't be afraid to speak up and decline. Later, you'll be glad you did.

During the interview, ask the employer questions about:

- Your duties and responsibilities
- Specific questions to your Leader
- Stability of the company
- Work environment and co-workers
- Level of stress involved in the position
- Any other concerns

Let's address each one in some detail.

Duties and Responsibilities:

Are you clear on your duties and responsibilities? If not, ask,

- Where the job fits into the organization?
- Is there a path for advancement?
- Is it clear who works for you?
- Is it clear who you work for, with and who works for you?

Specific questions to your Leader:

- What do you expect of the new person in the first 90-days?
- How do you measure job performance of your direct reports?
- How do you measure results and behavior?
- What're the most important skills you're looking for?
- Are there any major events or changes coming?
- What're your priorities for this position?
- How many people have held this position in the past 3-years?
- Why did they leave?

The Stability of the company:

- How stable is the company?
- Are sales or services increasing from year to year?
- Where do you see this company in five years?
- What's the company's market share?
- When was the last time anyone was laid off?
- Any new business opportunities expected?
- Who's their biggest competitor?
- Any litigation pending?

The Work Environment and your Co-workers:

- Ask employees what they like most (and least) about working here? (You may learn something you wouldn't have otherwise known.)
- Ssocial events, child care, flex time, and work from home?
- How well does the company care for their employees?
- Where do people go for lunch?
- What do people do if they get sick or need a day off?

Getting THE Call for Job Interviews and Offers

The level of stress involved with the position:
- Are there any employees to watch out for or stay away from?
- Any major crisis management events in the past?
- Any major stressful events coming up?
- Any work after 5 PM or on weekends?

Other concerns:

- Anything that makes you uncomfortable?
- People taking work home with them?
- Work on weekends or holidays?
- Any travel involved?
- Bad language or loud noises?
- Harassment and smoking?

WHAT QUESTIONS WILL THEY ASK YOU?

When the interview begins, here are some questions you'll be asked:

- Most commonly asked question
- What do you know about us?
- Negative questions
- Behavioral question
- What are your compensation expectations?
- What are your questions for us?

Let's address each one in some detail.

What's the most commonly asked question?

The most commonly asked question is, *Tell me about yourself*. So, expect it. Present your 30-second commercial along with any PAR stories that apply. Most of the time, this question is asked just to give the interviewer a chance to relax. So, be prepared for it. Know your strengths, use your PCF/BOE related PAR stories and tell how you can *add value* to your Leader's PCF/BOE goals.

"What do you know about us" type questions:

Similar Questions:

- Do you really want to work with us or do you just want a job?
- Did you do your homework and prepare for this interview?
- Do you have any clue what we do here and why?
- Why would you want to work for our company?
- What about our company interests you?

Do your research before the interview to give an appropriate answer. Discuss how your skills fill the needs of the job description. Use PAR stories.

How do I answer Negative Questions?

There are hundreds of possible negative questions that could be asked. The list is endless. For example, if asked, *what's your biggest weakness?* But, here's the process.

> ***First***, to say that you have no weaknesses, or you haven't made a mistake, or that you've not had a misunderstanding is a lie. You just screened yourself out for a lack of integrity. So, clearly answer the question. Pick an actual, true event from your past that was harmless and insignificant.
>
> ***Second***, tell the rest of the story; what did you learn as a result of the experience.

For example, if asked, *what is your greatest weakness?* You might respond with a pause and say;

> *"Probably my greatest weakness is patience. I just want to get things done right the first time. What I've learned to do over the years is to better communicate how much time is left and how important it is to get things completed on-time."*

So, now what's your greatest weakness? You don't have one. You had one, but you made it go away. You've *made lemonade out of lemons*.

You showed how to turn a weakness into strength. This is how to change a negative question into a positive answer.

Similar questions:

- People are always complaining. What do people complain about you?
- How do you feel about your former Leader or company?
- Why did you leave your previous job?
- What's you biggest mistake?

When asked why you left your previous job, stay away from emotions and judgments. State the facts *only*. Stay away from assumptions or your opinion of the facts. For example: If asked, "Why did you leave your last job?" you might respond with, "There was no room for upward mobility, or the position lacked challenge, or the company or industry was unstable or it was time to move on."

Refrain from criticizing a former supervisor. Be prepared to offer specific stories concerning both your transferable skills and your most outstanding achievements as they relate to the job description.

How do I answer Behavioral Questions?

Employers often ask behavioral questions to see how you behaved in certain situations from your past. As you answer, provide specific examples that show your thought process.

Similar questions:

- Describe the most recent situation where you were under pressure. How did you react?
- Describe your last major mistake. Why did it happen? What did you do about it?
- Describe your greatest success at work and tell me when it occurred?
- Tell me about a time when your ideas were rejected by your Leader? How did you work through the situation?

Use your PAR stories. They're looking for how you responded in this situation. Use stories that have a good response.

How do I answer questions about Compensation?

Understand the two primary rules of negotiating compensation;

RULE #1:
Whoever states a number first, loses!

Things you could say instead include:

> *"Compensation isn't a big issue for me. But, finding the right match is important. We can discuss compensation later."*

> *"I'm confident we can work out compensation later. Let's continue to see if I'm the right person for this job."*

> *"What was the range for my predecessor? If it's a new position, what range have you budgeted for this position?"*

Getting THE Call for Job Interviews and Offers

RULE #2:
Don't discuss compensation until you have the offer in writing.

Get the offer in writing, then, ask for time to consider it. After 24-48 hours, return to your Leader (not HR) to negotiate the details.

You may be a good talker, but a job interview is not a conversation; it's a competition. They're judging you on everything you say, don't say, and do. And, you should be judging them to see if this job is a good fit for you.

Check to ensure you've asked all your prepared questions or any other questions that came to mind during the interview.

WHAT SHOULD YOU DO DURING THE INTERVIEW?

Assess your Body Language:

Body language is an important tool you can use in a job interview. If you have a video or web camera, use it for your practice job interviews; otherwise a mirror will do, or get feedback from a friend. Hand and arm movements shouldn't be too large. Don't fiddle, shake your leg, or tap your fingers. This is unprofessional and may distract your potential employer. Your posture is relaxed, but alert. Don't slouch. If you look bored, the interviewer may assume you'd be bored in the job.

Communicate desire, interest, and enthusiasm!

Most people do this with their face, hand-gestures, posture, and voice. Be yourself. Your potential employer knows that you're nervous, but try not to make it so obvious that it becomes a distraction. In a study conducted at UCLA, they found that 93% of our daily verbal communication has nothing to do with the words we speak. When we speak, 55% of our message is communicated by our body language (posture, gestures, eye contact), 38% by our tonality (your tone of voice) and 7% by the content of your words.

Also, your facial expressions communicate several different emotions like:

Anger, concentration, contempt, desire, disgust, excitement, fear, happiness, sadness, confusion, and surprise.

Make sure your facial expressions and body language show concentration, desire, excitement, and happiness.

If you're trying to show desire, interest, and enthusiasm, make sure you tell your face!

Dress for Success:

It's easy, dress your best! You wouldn't wear torn jeans to a wedding, nor would you wear cargo shorts to an interview. Remember, looking professional means looking respectable. It's best to error on the side of formality.

While many offices allow their employees to dress casually on a day-to-day basis, your interview is a time to make a professional first impression with your appearance. There will be plenty of casual Fridays to take advantage of after you're hired.

Have faith! If you didn't have something they needed, you wouldn't have been invited to the interview. Relax, have fun, and spend some quality time determining if this position is a good fit.

Personal Grooming is part of Dressing for Success:

Your breath is important! Don't chew gum during an interview. Breath mints or spray will work just fine. Be sure to freshen up before your interview, but don't overwhelm your potential employer with your favorite perfume or cologne. Hair is kept simple. When it comes to makeup – less is more. Take extra time to look great and it will be one less thing that stands between you and your dream job.

Take your time before answering:

Take your time. There's no rush! You're going to be asked some questions and there is some skill needed to answer them well. Don't ramble. Concise answers with strong PAR stories are better than disorganized babble. Focus on the job description's transferrable skills. Connect your PAR stories to those transferrable skills.

Explain how your transferrable skills contribute to your leader's PCF/BOE goals. Demonstrate desire, interest, and enthusiasm. Look the interviewer in the eye when you're answering.

Gather your thoughts. If you need a minute to collect your thoughts to answer a specific question, feel free to say, *I need to think about that for a moment...* or *that's a great question, one I hadn't thought of before.*

Relax and have fun:

Most of us have heard of R&R and know that it stands for *Rest and Relaxation*. However, few people know that rest is for the body and relaxation is for the mind. So, how do you relax your mind? It's simple; stress reduction.

Everyone reacts to stress differently. Some people verbally express their stress to help cope with their mounting tasks. Others draw inward, choosing to process their stress internally and plan their course of action.

Genetics, also, play a part in how you handle stress, because of overactive or underactive stress responses, one's own life experiences, and/or a history of anxiety disorder, according to Mayo Clinic research. Other than the obvious stress reducers like exercise, laughter and/or a hobby, here are a few more suggestions.

Just breathe:

Shallow, chest breathing, the kind most of us do involuntarily, activates the sympathetic nervous system. Its purpose is to prepare your body for a fight-or-flight response by raising your heart rate and blood pressure, dilating your pupils, and increasing your sweat gland production. These are good for running from bears, but bad for doing well in a job interview. Instead, concentrate on deep breathing from your abdomen. Slow inhalation and exhalation can help reset your body's equilibrium and lower your naturally occurring stress hormones.

Clench and release:

Sometimes used as a meditation exercise, tightening, and releasing your body's muscles is a proven relaxation technique. Clenching one part of your body at a time, such as arms or legs, or your entire body all at once and holding that pose for several seconds helps release excess tension in your arms, shoulders, back and feet.

How can you make a good First Impression?

Look the person in the eye as you offer your right hand for a handshake. Shake their hand firmly, but easily. Smile at the same time, and say something enthusiastic like, *Hi, Mr. Byrnes. It's nice to meet you!* As you walk into the office make some small talk – weather, or how great the lobby looks.

Avoid discussing politics, race, religion, sex, or humor.

Small talk will establish a positive rapport, and the rest of the interview will feel more natural and less like you're being grilled.

Focus:

Your job is to sell your future potential. So, know your skills well enough to do this effectively. Once you figure that out, discuss how your skills match the needs of the employer. Connecting your skills with the company's needs (as described in the job description) is the best way to get hired. But, above all, be authentic! If an employer doesn't perceive you have a sincere interest in their organization, they can't be sure you'll be committed to their success.

Establish Rapport:

One of the most important things you can do at the beginning of any interview (or any other first meeting with a stranger) is to establish rapport.

To establish rapport, you'll need three things:

- *Power of observation:* When you first walk into the interview room (normally an office), look around for pictures, plaques, certificates, awards, or anything of a personal nature. For example: A picture of children. This picture is a perfect transition into asking questions about their family. People love to talk about their family.

- *Personal questions:* Topics of conversation initially should focus on family, sports, the weather, or anything else you've observed in the office. Topics to steer away from are humor, sex, race, religion, and politics.

- *Mirroring and Matching:* People tend to warm up to people who are like them. Mirroring and matching is a very simple process of observing someone's mannerisms and speech and mirroring back to them what you see. For example: If the interviewer was talking slower than you normally talk – consider slowing your rate of speech.

Avoid Self-Deprecating Comments

The biggest problem my clients faced during role-play interviews was that they were self-deprecating; they tended to undervalue their abilities. It wasn't until I showed it to them on video that they understood. They would say things that cast doubt in the interviewer's mind.

For example: I'd ask him a simple question like, *how good are you at basic math?* He would say, *Actually, I hate math and it was my worst subject in school.* Ops! Not only did he give me too much information that I didn't ask for – but now I'm doubtful as to his ability to do the job. It was as if he thought he was getting extra points for being overly honest, when just the opposite was true.

Assuming he could balance his checking account and use a calculator and/or a computer, he could have said, *I have good basic math skills*. If they needed to know exactly how good his math skills were, they'd give him a basic math test.

Stop screening yourself out by your self-deprecating comments. Tell the interviewer what you can do, not what you can't do!

Also, if asked to rate yourself from 1-10 on any skill listed on your resume, if you can't rate yourself a 9 or above, do yourself a favor - **Stay Home!** This is not the time to be humble, especially when they're asking you for a self-assessment.

Your job is to sell your future potential. Know your skills well enough to do this effectively. Once you figure that out, you can apply your skills to their needs. Discussing your transferrable skills, using PAR stories, against the company's needs, as described in their job description, is the best way to get hired.

But, above all, be authentic! If an employer doesn't perceive you have a sincere interest in their organization, they can't be sure you'll be committed to their success.

If the job description is vague or it changes during the interview (a frequent occurrence), ask the interviewer for the most important skills they're seeking. Then, use your PAR stories to focus on those skills.

Getting THE Call for Job Interviews and Offers

Ask yourself these questions during the interview:
- Will I be challenged to grow in this position?
- Do I like the people I've met so far?
- Can I work with my Leader?
- Is the compensation fair?
- How many people have held this position in the past 3 years?
- Any major events or changes coming?
- Can I deal with the stress level?

WHAT SHOULD YOU DO AT THE END?

Closing is a term used to describe the process of securing a job offer. Knowing how to successfully close or wrap up an interview can be the difference between getting invited back for another interview, getting an offer, or getting screened out. You want to leave an impression that you're the right person for the job, which requires a combination of equal parts skill and personality.

Ask for their Perception of your Candidacy

The questions below require your interviewer to give you an immediate indication if he thinks you're right for the job. Ask,

"Do you have any concerns about me filling this position?"

or

"Do you think I'm a good fit for this position?"

While it's possible your interviewer could take this opportunity to voice his objections, it's better to identify his concerns so you can address them or to learn from them to strengthen your next interview. Be prepared to address any anticipated objections or concerns.

Do everything you can to mitigate their concerns by offering additional information before you depart.

Ask about the Next Step

This question is critical to a successful close. It's important for you to know the next step and it prompts your interviewer to immediately consider your candidacy.

Ask when they anticipate making a Final Decision

This establishes the period for your follow up call (before he makes his final decision). If possible, without sounding too pushy, try to get a fixed date.

Express your appreciation:

Ask for your interviewer's business card. You'll need this contact information to later send a thank you note. It also shows that you're professional, organized and plan on following-up. A firm handshake, with *strong eye-contact* and a *smile* at the beginning and end of an interview can further create an impression.

WHAT SHOULD YOU DO AFTER EACH INTERVIEW?

Conduct your own review of what happened:

Take some quiet time to reflect on the interview, by answering the following questions:

- What question could you not answer (or struggled)?
- What question made you uncomfortable?
- Did they raise any objections or concerns?
- What did you learn and what can you do better next time?

If so, work on strengthening any weaknesses. This will help you prepare for the next interview, because there will be more!

Be Self-Correcting!

Send a handwritten thank you note:

While an email "thank you" note is okay, a handwritten thank you note displays more time and effort and allows you to further personalize your appeal and impression.

Note: If you want to stand out and be remembered, send a hand written thank you note via USPS. For maximum effect, use a black, wide-tipped pen on nice 6 X 9 personalized stationary (From the desk of…), and add your favorite motivational quote at the bottom. If your handwriting isn't legible, have someone else write it for you.

Follow up with a phone call:

Make a follow up call to your potential Leader before the date he said he would decide. Reaffirm your desire, interest, and enthusiasm. If he's not available, leave a professional voice mail message showing your desire, interest, and enthusiasm.

Failing to follow up sends the wrong message. Do the right thing!

Remember, the person they selected (if not you) may turn down their offer or may not work out and quit after 30-days. You want to be remembered for all the right reasons. So, always do the right thing, follow up! And, if you're not selected for the position, it's their loss – not yours.

Interviewing is a numbers game!
Some will, Some won't, So what, Next!
Keep going! Don't let rejection stop you!

Consider the Pre-Emptive Approach:

Based upon your level of confidence and experience, you could start the interview by making a presentation.

You could anticipate their questions and present to them exactly what you've done for your previous employers to enhance their PCF/BOE like:

- Photos
- Samples of work you've completed
- Diagrams, sketches
- Digital copies on a laptop
- Previous performance reports
- Awards, commendations, recognition

Also, don't leave any documents with the interviewer. Someone might just copy your work and then not hire you. The intent here is to knock their socks off!

Caution: Make sure whatever you're presenting does not violate any company secrets, proprietary methods, or intellectual property.

CHAPTER 9:
NEGOTIATING TO RECEIVE THE HIGHEST OFFER

"The most important trip you may take in life is meeting people half way.
- Henry Boyle

WHAT'S THE BEST COMPENSATION FOR YOU?

The best compensation is the highest they're willing to pay.

How do you know the highest they're willing to pay? There's only one way; negotiate like you mean it.

There's a process you must go through, in the right sequence, at the right time, to find and receive the highest compensation they can afford.

Do employers offer the highest compensation they can afford in their initial offer? Usually, No! The only way to know their ceiling is to ASK!

Your goal is to receive the highest compensation for your actual value added or, at least, to be compensated fairly. The employer's goal is to hire the best talent for the least price.

The best time to negotiate compensation is after you have a written offer letter and before you sign it. If you attempt to negotiate before you have their initial offer, you have no *leverage*.

Without *leverage*, if you give them a salary number before you receive their offer, one of two things could happen:

- The number could be <u>too high</u>, they could say they will consider it, and never call you back. Why, because you were too expensive.

- The number could be <u>too low</u>, they could say they will consider it, and never call you back. Why, because you were too low. Maybe you really didn't have the skills they thought you had.

Play it cool and wait for the right time to negotiate -
after you have their offer in writing.

What's in a Total Compensation Package?

A *Total Compensation Package* normally includes:

- **Salary** like cash wages and how frequently they are paid. It could also include raises, bonuses, or other incentives.
- **Benefits** like medical, dental, eye glass care, retirement (401 contribution), paid vacation, paid holidays, etc.
- **Perks** like a company car, expense account, corner office, executive assistant, reserved parking, relocation, etc.

If you're moving to a new area, will the new employer pay for all your moving costs, a house hunting trip for you and your wife, temporary housing, as needed, etc. If not, you'll have some serious no non-reimbursable, out-of-pocket, moving related expenses. Also, if you are in sales, it could include, a company car, expense account, company credit card, and a host of other things.

WHAT'S "LEVERAGE"?

Leverage is the power to produce a maximum advantage in a negotiation.

Your *Leverage* in the negotiation is a function tow things; their *Urgency* and your *Perceived Value Added.*

Your Leverage = Their Urgency + Your Perceived Value Added

What's their Urgency?

Their Urgency is a function of how quickly or urgently they must fill a position.

To estimate their *Urgency* in your situation, answer this question:

- How soon must they fill the position and why?
- How long has this position been vacant and why?
- How many others are they interviewing?
- Is this a *new* position or why did the previous person leave?
- Who is currently doing the work for this position?

Important: Someone's currently performing the duties for this position and it's probably your leader. Your leader can't wait to get someone on-board so he can unload these duties. This *Urgency* gives you *Leverage*.

What if there's no Urgency on the part of the employer?

If there is no *Urgency* from the employer, the only *Leverage* you have is your *Perceived Value Added*.

What's your Perceived Value-Added?

Your *Perceived Value-Added* is the employer's perception of your ability to make a positive impact on their organization. Your *Perceived Value-Added* is quite simply the sum of everything you bring to the table (like your knowledge, skills, experience, achievements, attitude, relationships, character, and balance) that has contributed, in some measurable and significant way, to the achievement of your leader's goals.

Their perceptions of you comes from:

- Your resume
- Your reputation (their checking and research of you),
- The additional skills you bring that they were not looking for
- How you answer questions and sell yourself during their interviewing process
- The other skills you bring to the position include additional education, training, and certifications, your contacts, more experience, etc. Many of these items will only be revealed during the interview process.

Your achievements are found in your resume and are reinforced by how well you present yourself.

To estimate your *Perceived Value-Added* in your situation, answer this question:

- How bad do they want you?
- Are they bragging or trying to sell you on the company?
- Are they saying things like, *you'll really like it here* or *when you start working here...?*

- What do you bring to the position that was not asked for in the job description – like additional education, training, certification, contacts, or additional experience?
- How strong and relevant are your achievement as they relate to their Job Description?

WHAT ARE THE RULES WHEN NEGOTIATING?

Here are the primary rules for negotiating total compensation:

RULE #1:
Whoever states a number first, LOSES!

When someone asks you for your salary requirements or a range, do not give them a number. Instead, respond by using one of the following:

> *"Compensation isn't a big issue for me. But, finding the right match is important. We can discuss compensation later."*

> *"I'm confident we can work out compensation later. Let's continue to see if I'm the right person for this job."*

> *"What was the range for my predecessor? If it's a new position, what range have you budgeted for this position?"*

RULE #2:
Don't discuss compensation until you have the offer in writing.

Get the offer in writing, then, ask for time to consider it. After 24-48 hours, return to your Leader (not HR) to negotiate the details.

You may be a good talker, but a job interview is not a conversation; it's a competition. They're judging you on everything you say, don't say, and do. And, you should be judging them to see if this job is a good fit for you.

Check to ensure you've asked all your prepared questions or any other questions that came to mind during the interview. Strongest *Leverage* occurs after you have the written offer and before you accept the offer.

RULE #3:
Do not ask for things from someone who has no authority to grant.

Asking your manager for things not covered by their company insurance provider (like Eye Glass Care) is not something he can grant-without changing the insurance package for the entire company. Also, do not attempt to negotiate with Human Resources. They have no authority to grant anything. You need to be talking to you direct manager or his manager.

WHAT ARE THE GAMBITS (OR PLAYS)?

A Gambit is a trick or play that you can use to either counter their gambit or to put yourself into a better negotiating position. Your goal is to receive the highest compensation for your actual *value added* or, at least, to be compensated fairly. The employer's goal is to hire the best talent for the least price.

What Gambits will the Employer Play?

Their Gambit 1:

The tactic they will play against you is that they need your final salary numbers to put together their offer.

Your counter should be;

> *"I know that you'll make me a fair offer. Should I wait around for the offer letter or should I come back tomorrow, or can you email it to me?"*

Your goal is to ask for 48 hours to consider their offer and to get out of there with a written offer.

Their Gambit 2:

They can also say, *We're offering $55,000, will that work for you?*

Your counter should be;

> *That's fine. I'm interested in the entire package. I'd like to see your offer letter, is that okay?"*

Do not begin to negotiate or give them a number. Negotiating only begins after you receive their written offer.

Then, as for 48 hours to consider the offer and go home.

Their Gambit 3:

During your first visit, you will be asked to fill out an Employment Application, which will normally ask you to answer the following questions:

> Have you ever files for bankruptcy?
>
> Do you have any felonies or convictions?
>
> What's your salary history?

<u>Your Counter:</u> Answer all questions honestly. Do not leave anything blank. Just know that your past salary represents the floor of the negotiations-not the ceiling.

What Gambit can you Play?

Your Gambit 1: Put yourself in the position of your employer

What objections do you expect? What response do you have for these objections? Many people are afraid or too proud to negotiate and/or ask for anything. The better you negotiate, the more you'll receive.

Your Gambit 2: Ask for more than you need.

When you ask for anything, your manager can answer three different ways. He can say, Yes, No, or he can split-the-difference and give you half of what you asked for. Anticipate this. If you're asking for a signing bonus and you want $5,000, ask for $10,000 instead. This way your manager can think he's winning the negotiation by granting you $5,000.

Getting THE Call for Job Interviews and Offers

Your Gambit 3: Ask for things that reduce your out-of-pocket costs.

Salary isn't everything! What you get to keep is far more important than how much you make.

By that I mean that it's your job to do all you can to reducing your out-of-pocket expenses. If you're smart, you can ask for things that have little value to them, but have great value to you. Here's an example.

What kind of company are you joining? Most companies either sell products, or provide services to their customers.

If the company sells a product:

If the company sells a product; you can ask for free stuff or stuff at a reduced price.

Example: I once had a client who was negotiating with one of the largest grocery chains in the region. When they reached the ceiling on salary, my client asked for free groceries for his family for a year. They agreed.

If the company provides services:

If the company provides services, can you get free or reduced price services.

Example: A client was interviewing with a company that rental cars. My client asked for the use of a rental car of his choosing as part of his contract. They agreed.

What if the company does neither?

If so, use Gambit 4!

Your Gambit 4: Ask for incentives based on your Key Performance Indicators (KPIs).

If the company does neither, ask to link additional compensation (Bonus) to your future performance (your KPIs) with the performance review after a specified time (after 90-days, or six months)

You should already know what your KPI are from previous experience. If not, ask for them during your interview.

Remember what my client wrote in my introduction:

"Thanks to Ed, I learned the secrets of running a successful job search and in only two weeks I found my career position. I actually had two offers from which to choose and was able to leverage that situation into a 10% raise plus a bonus, all before I ever worked a day. Thanks doesn't seem enough." – William S., San Diego, CA

Did my client get a 10% raise and a signing bonus because he deserved it? No, he got it because he asked for it! And, so can you!

"You do not get what you want. You get what you negotiate."
- Harvey Mackay

I would also add:

You don't get what you deserve, you get what you negotiate!

Example: I had a client who interviewed with a company that produced and sold heavy lift equipment like fork lifts. Here, he needed to be a little more creative. He asked his manager to link a 10% Bonus to his *Key Performance Indicators* (KPI), that he created.

Why not link a salary increase, or a bonus, or both to achieving, maintaining, or exceeding your KPIs?

If you don't achieve them, no big deal. Renegotiate them in a year. What do you have to lose?

Your Gambit 5: Take time to consider the offer.

When a final offer is extended, if it's not enough, thank the employer and ask for time to consider the offer (24-48 hours is customary).

Then, come back and try asking one more time by asking, *I know you said that you couldn't go any higher in terms of salary, but is there anything else you can do to make this offer more attractive?* (Like more vacation, signing bonus, free access to…, etc.)

Your Gambit 6: What else can they offer to "sweeten the pie"?

At the end of the negotiation, especially if things did not go your way, ask, *What else can we do to make this deal better?* Now, be silent! Let them figure out how to better incentivize you. Also, you don't have refuse the offer yet. You could recommend that your manager take 48 hours to think about it. Then, decide.

Your Gambit 7: Use silence for consideration

During negotiations, in response to an offer, restate the offer, sit quietly, and silently count to 10. This technique may also prompt the employer to justify the offer, which could continue the negotiation process, or it could lead to a better offer.

Gambit 8: Walk away!

Don't be afraid to walk away. By that I mean, respectfully decline. Don't burn any bridges. If your feel their offer to be unfair, do not accept the offer and move on.

CONDUCT A SALARY & COL SURVEY

Compensation is always a trade-off. You have something to sell; your *Perceived Value Added*, and the employer should fairly compensate you for it. Any good employee should be worth 4-5 times their annual salary.

Conduct a Salary Survey:

Get on the Internet and review pay surveys to see what the average pay is for your position and industry (like *Survey Monkey*).

Conduct a Cost of Living Survey:

You can't estimate a fair salary without assessing the cost of living for where you and your family will be living. Especially if you're are moving from the mid-west to either the East or West Coast. A salary of $80, 000 may be great for Kansas City, but you'll twice that salary on either coast.

To gauge the cost of living outside your area, visit *Salary.com*, use their *Cost of Living Wizard*.

CONDUCT A NEEDS ASSESSMENT

What are the Employer's needs?

As you prepare to negotiate, find out the employer's needs (focus on their Job Description) and try to meet them without losing sight of your own goals.

Here are a few questions to help you better determine the employer's needs:

- What is the employer asking for in their description of the job? Do you meet all their requirements? Do you exceed their requirements?
- Are you a good match? What else can you do for the employer that exceeds what they're asking for?
- Have you done your research on the company?
- Have you read all the news you can find?
- Have you talked to other employees before your first interview?
- Have you uncovered other needs within the company during your interviews?

This isn't rocket science! Their problems, concerns, and needs are out there. You just need to dig a little!

What are your needs?

Here are a few questions to help you better determine your needs:

- What're you looking for in terms of pay and benefits?
- What does the organization want from you?
- What can you offer the organization?
- What does the industry generally pay for your skills (web search)?

Getting THE Call for Job Interviews and Offers

As you identify your goals, list things that you want included, such as:
- Not working on weekends
- Earning $XXX, 000 a year or $XX per hour
- Sick leave
- Performance review within 3-months for wage increase
- Money for relocation
- Signing bonus
- Six weeks of vacation
- Work from home

Evaluate your goals and rank-order them from most important at the top, to lease important at the bottom. Prioritize your goals and prepare options you can suggest if your preferred request is not accepted.

Anticipate areas that might present problems, and then list several alternatives to resolve these issues. Throughout the negotiation, remember to be open and honest. Negotiations should leave both parties feeling satisfied with the outcome.

Gambit 9: Answer their question with a question.

If they keep pushing you to give them a number or a range, just ask,

> *What the salary range for this position?*
>
> *or*
>
> *What did the previous person receive as a salary?*

Gambit 10: Only discuss salary specifics with real recruiters (not HR)

How you answer salary questions, depends on who is calling:

- If you're talking to a <u>recruiting company</u> (not from the employer's company), or an independent recruiter, answer all their questions honestly (tell him your pay range).

    If you're talking to someone from the <u>employer's company</u> (like Human Resources or an in-company recruiter), don't answer questions about salary, other than to say,

I'm very open and flexible.
Compensation's negotiable.
I'm just looking for a good fit.

YOUR FIRST INTERVIEW

What's an Employment Application?

During your first visit, they will ask you to fill out a job application which will ask you to answer the following questions:

- Have you ever files for bankruptcy?
- Do you have any felonies or convictions?
- What's your salary history?

Their Gambit 1:

On the application, you may be asked for a salary history. I don't recommend you leave the question blank. Just know that your past salary is the floor of the negotiations for you-not the ceiling.

Once the application is complete, you'll begin a round-robin of interviews with various employees. Their job is to rate you on how well you fit the position in question.

Now, it's time to ask questions and tell your story.

Remember: Your *Perceived Value Added* is quite simply the employer's perception of everything you bring to the table (like your knowledge, skills, experience, achievements, attitude, relationships, character, and balance).

Your job during the interviewing is to sell yourself; to do all you can to increase your Perceived Value Added by how well you tell your PAR stories.

During the interview, the most important things you can do are:

- *Ask questions:* If you ask permission to ask questions, you'll lay a foundation for agreement and likely receive a complete answer. Ask open-ended questions to gain information and build a relationship. Open-ended questions typically begin with who, what, when, where, and why. Use closed-ended questions (questions that encourage short answers, such as *Yes* or *No*) when you want to gain a concession or confirm a deal point.

- *Be a good listener:* The more information you get, the better able you'll be to uncover their needs and it'll be easier for you to show how you're able to meet those needs. Take notes and record the names of the employees you've met.

- *Paraphrase to ensure understanding:* Restate what you were told (their response) to make sure you understand it correctly.

- *Take notes:* Notes will help all parties recall what has already been discussed or decided. Be sure to get all offers in writing.

- *Emphasize your value added:* Explain how you can contribute to their goals. Use your PAR Stories.

- *Be flexible:* Take the attitude of *I'm just working out the details*. When asked how much money you're looking for, remember whoever states a number first, loses. Make sure it's not you.

Instead, say:

> **"Compensation is not a big issue for me. But, finding the right match is important. We can discuss compensation later."**
>
> **"I'm confident we can work out compensation later. Let's continue to see if I'm the right person for this job."**
>
> **"What was the range for my predecessor? If it's a new position, what range have you budgeted for this position?"**

Your purpose of a job interview is to find a good match and to receive an offer in writing. This book is designed to help you better negotiate that offer.

Their Gambit 2:

The tactic they will play against you is that they will tell you need your final salary numbers to put together their offer.

Your counter should be:

> *"I know that you'll make me a fair offer. Should I wait around for the offer letter or should I come back tomorrow, or can you email it to me?"*

Their Gambit 3:

They can also say, *We're offering $55,000, will that work for you?*

Your counter should be:

> *That's fine. I'm interested in the entire package. I'd like to see your offer letter, is that okay?"*

Do not begin to negotiate or give them a number. Negotiating only begins after you receive their written offer and have had a chance to review it. Then, ask for 48 hours to consider the offer and go home.

What's an Offer Letter?

An *Offer Letter* is a simple employment contract stating your:

- Job Title
- Start date
- How often you'll be paid
- What they are willing to offer you, and
- A vague reference to their benefit package (requiring numerous questions to pin down what it includes).
- A place for you to sign signifying your acceptance of their offer

Before you Depart:

Before you depart, set a time with your direct manager to return to discuss the offer in 48 hours. Do not discuss the offer when you first receive it. Don't say anything other than to ask for 48 hours to consider the offer. If married, you will need this time to discuss the offer with your spouse.

Note: For more specifics on how to ace your interview, please see *Interview Like You Mean It:* How to interview strong enough to receive a job offer.

AFTER YOU RECEIVE THEIR OFFER

Carefully assess their benefit package

When home, with your written offer in hand, take the time to assess the specifics of their benefit package with your spouse. Compare their benefit package with your previous employer package.

If the benefit package was not fully explained during the visit, look it up on their web site (or call HR and ask your questions and, if needed, ask them to email you something in hard copy so you can review it.)

Go through the benefits carefully. You don't want any surprises later. Does it include medical, dental, eye glass care? Does it include all your family members? What part of the benefit package is missing or unacceptable to you?

After you and your spouse have discussed reviewed the offer, assume that you find yourself in this situation.

Situation: Let's assume that you liked the offer, however, there were a few concerns:

> *Their offer was $55,000. That was the salary you had from your last employer. You'd like to see if this is the highest offer they can afford.*
>
> *The vacation package only offered 2 weeks of paid vacation. You would prefer 3 weeks.*

Prepare for the Final Negotiation Meeting

After reviewing their offer with your spouse, return to meet with your manager to discuss the offer. Ensure you speak to your direct manager, not HR. Human Resources cannot negotiate anything.

Their Gambit:

The common tactic employers use is to have you meet with HR.

Your Counter:

Insist on discussing the offer with your direct manager before accepting it because you have questions only your manager can answer.

During the meeting with your new manager, *John*, here's a sample dialog to use during your meeting:

As a review, a good Request, has three components:

- Topic: Concerning the starting salary....
- Justification: Based on my having an MBA....
- Question: I would like to ask, is it possible.......? Or, is there anything else you can do?

Important: Every time you ask for something, you need to justify your request. If you have a good reason, your chances are good that your request will be approved.

DURING THE NEGOTIATION (OR NEXT) MEETING

Start out by saying, *John, I appreciate your offer, but I have a few concerns. Is this a good time to discuss them?*

Start by addressing each issue, one at a time

- *Topic: On the issue of salary, I'm grateful for the offer of $55,000*
- *Justification: Based on the survey research I've done, the range in this region for this position is $60 – 70, 000.*
- *Question: Let me ask this, is there anything we can do to get into this range? Is that possible?*

Your manager can answer each question one of three ways; either Yes, No, or let's split-the-difference.

Your manager declined your request, move on to the next issue on your list.

My next concern is ....

- *Topic: On the issue of two weeks of paid vacation.*
- *Justification: Based on my five years of experience in your industry and my ability to hit the ground running in terms of ......*
- *Question: Let me ask this, could I get 3 weeks of paid vacation. Is that possible?*

Your manager agrees.

At the end of all your issues, return to the items your manager declined.

On the salary issue, you can always ask for a Starting Bonus.

- *Topic: "John, I'd like to revisit the salary issue again. I understand your concerns about keep the salary the same for all new employees,*
- *Justification: As I mentioned, based on the survey research I've done, the range in the region for this position is $60 – 70, 000. And, I know I'm worth that.*

Getting THE Call for Job Interviews and Offers

- *Question: Let me ask this, could I receive at $10,000 signing bonus-in lieu of a salary increase? Is it possible?*

Always ask for more than you want. For example, if you want a $5,000 signing bonus, ask for a $10,000 bonus.

Note: You're being judged on your transferrable skills. How well you negotiate tells them that you have another valuable transferable skill; negotiating.

Warning: Be careful. Play it cool. If you appear desperate, your ability to negotiate will be greatly diminished. If they ask, *are you looking at other companies?* Or *are you considering other offers,* say, I'd *rather not say.*

WHAT IF IT DOESN'T GO YOUR WAY?

As you know, life isn't perfect.

Negotiations normally fall apart when you don't have the Leverage you thought you had.

There are several reasons your manager may not approve any of your requests. You may not have the *Leverage* you thought you had. They may already be at the ceiling of what they can offer you right now (future potential)

Important: If your overall compensation is less that what you had last, why would you want to accept their offer? Don't be afraid to walk away, respectfully, don't burn any bridges. If they do not recognize your true value added, do you really want to work for them. If they are not fairly compensating you for all you bring to them, respectfully decline.

TRAINING: To better understand how to negotiate in a high-stakes, high-stress environment watch the movie, ***Draft Day***, a 2014 American sports drama film starring *Kevin Costner*. The premise revolves around the general manager of the Cleveland Browns (Costner) deciding what to do after his team acquires the number one draft pick in the upcoming National Football League draft. Then, conduct a group discussion answering these questions: Why did Costner hesitate when trying to hire the number one rated college quarterback. What gambits did Costner use that were used against him. How can you use what you've learned from the movie?

Discover the Job Searching SECRETS Employer's Don't Want You to Know.

CHAPTER 10:
ASSESSING YOUR JOB SEARCH

"Success is to be measured not so much by the position that one has reached in life as by the obstacles which he has overcome."
- Booker T. Washington

If you don't have a way to record and track your actions and communications during your search – you'll quickly become overwhelmed and lose opportunities that were yours for the taking.

Here's the system I created with my clients.

Search Management System Instructions

- *Purpose:* To provide instructions concerning actions that will lead to your success during your search.
- *Frequency:* If you'll take these actions on a daily, weekly, and monthly basis, you'll be successful.

- *Accountability:* Every week, assess your progress using the *Seeds of Success Activity Log* to help you achieve your goals more quickly.

    Goals: Your goal is to find a new position as soon as possible. However, your intermediate goal is to get as many advice meetings or job interviews, as possible. So, the question remains, how can I get lots of these meetings/interviews? And, the best answer is to sow and nourish the Seeds of Success. The Seeds are the actions that will bring you ultimate success because they attack 100% of the job market.

Interviews and advice meetings are the fruits of your labor.
If you'll plant the seeds (take the actions) and nourish
them (follow up), you'll be successful.

Track Your Goals vs. Results

On the *Seeds of Success Activity Log* below, on the left, begin by putting a number representing your weekly goal; the number of times you expect to execute this task per week. Now, go out and execute your plan.

Do as many of these actions as you can, each day and each week, and you will be successful. Then, at the end of the week, record the results (the actual number of each action you've completed) on the right.

Your goal is to sow as many seeds as you
can in every category, every day.

Use this format to record your weekly goals on the *left* and your results on the *right*.

Sample Weekly Seeds of Success Activity Log:

GOAL VS. RESULT

Goal	Activity	Result
	30-Second Commercial	
	Advertised Jobs Letters	
	PIK Letters	
	Advice Letters	
	Approach Letters	
	Emerging Opportunity Letters	
	Classmate Letters	
	Calls, Advertised Jobs Letters	
	Calls, PIK Letters	
	Calls, Advice Letters	
	Calls, Approach Letters	
	Calls, Emerging Opportunity Letters	
	Calls to Classmates	
	Visits to Target Companies	
	Association, Society, Club Meetings	
	Social Events	
	Conventions & Seminars	
	Chamber Meetings	
	Let's Do Lunch	
	Networking Cards	
	Resume on Web	
	Advice Meetings	

Take Massive Action!

The name of the game now is how many seeds can I sow each day, each week, each month? Take Massive Action! Your initial goal is a minimum of 10 per week on all *Seeds of Success*, except your 30-second commercial, which is to be done several times daily. Then, build from there. Keep track of your letters and follow up calls!

Follow up is critical to your success!

Perform these Actions Consistently!

After you've created your Special Purpose resumes and all your letters, ensure you perform these important activities consistently. Add these activities to your calendar.

- *Daily (End of Day):* Record all actions you took today on your Excel spreadsheet (for follow-up later). Don't trust your memory! Plan your activities for tomorrow. Who will you call? Who (which target company) will you go visit?

- *Weekly:* Record your *Seeds of Success Activity Log* for the week: Be accountable to yourself for the massive action you take every day. Don't worry about the results. You have no control over the results. Focus on what you do control; your thoughts, words, and actions!!! Assess your actions using your *Seeds of Success Activity Log*. Don't focus too much on results initially because this will take time. Focus on taking *massive action* to plant the *Seeds of Success*. Keep the faith and know that the more seeds you sow (action) and cultivate (follow up), the greater the harvest (results) will be over time. Also, check the web site of every company on your *Target List* for employment opportunities.

- *Monthly:* Revisit all job bank sites every 30 days and make one small change to your resume so that future employers have a better chance of viewing your resume. Many employers won't look at resumes that have been posted for 30 days or more. If you refresh your resume, now all new employers will see your resume.

Keep Track of Your Communications

To keep track of all your incoming and outgoing communications (so you don't forget to follow up), I recommend one simple Excel spreadsheet with a tabbed work sheet for each of these categories:

- PIK (Friends, family, social events, college alumni, sponsors)
- Target Companies (Advice and Approach letters and visits)
- Job Sites (Recruiters, Job Banks, Temp/Staffing)
- Social Networks (Facebook, LinkedIn.com, Twitter)
- Advertised Jobs (All jobs applied for on web and newspaper)
- Emerging Opportunities (All letters and follow up calls)
- Other (Conventions, Seminars, Workshops, Associations, Societies, Clubs, Chamber, Job Fairs)

Each tabbed work sheet should have three columns: *Initial Action*, *Follow up Action*, and *Results*.

Each of these three columns should have two columns: *Date*, *Action*.

Don't rely on your memory or little slips of paper to keep track of your actions and results.

Get serious and close out your daily actions and results at the end of every day. If you fail to keep track of your actions, you'll quickly lose control of your search, forget to follow up, and miss opportunities that were yours for the taking.

Persist and Be Successful!

If you continue taking massive action, you'll achieve your goal. It's no longer a question of if you're going to make it, but when.

Press On

*"Nothing in the world can take the place of persistence. Talent will not; nothing is more common than unsuccessful men with talent. Genius will not; unrewarded genius is almost a proverb. Education will not; the world is full of educated derelicts. Persistence and Determination are **Omnipotent**."- Charles Swindoll*

Understand that the more seeds you sow (action) and cultivate (follow up), the greater your harvest (results) over time. As you exercise your personal power, your job search will turn into interviews and offers. Changing what you think about, will change what you say and how you act, which will shape the reality of everything around you.

Success in your search will be a direct result of the massive action you take every day. Get out there! you can do this!

CHAPTER 11:
CHANGING CAREERS?

"I'm Proud to Be an American, where at least I know I'm free"
- Lee Greenwood

To my Brothers and Sisters in Arms, thank you for your loyal service to our Country.

Making the transition to civilian life will require a few adjustments. In addition to using everything in this guide to give yourself a competitive advantage, I recommend that you;

Change how you talk:

Drop the *Sir*, and *Hooah* and all the military jargon and pick up the jargon of your new profession. Change your voicemail; delete all military references and make it professional. Drop the phrase, *in the military*... Instead use, *in the past*... When answering a phone just say, *Hello*.

Change how you look:

Let your hair grow longer. Stay physically fit. Invest in some nice clothing; no shiny shoes or buttons on your lapel.

Change your resume:

Stop listing what you were responsible for; no one cares. List what you and your unit achieved, maintained, or exceeded based upon the military's *Band of Excellence* (BOE). Use transferrable skills like led, managed, directed, supervised, coordinated, and facilitated and list the details: # people involved, degree of difficulty, problems resolved, BOE, recognition received. Add security clearance. Civilians are associates, team members or employees, not personnel.

Example: Instead of, *Responsible for deploying an Infantry Platoon to Iraq,*

> Add, *Led a 25-member team that moved from Texas to Iraq, with 9 vehicles (plus weapons, radios, ...), traveling 500 miles via rail to Galveston, 3700 miles via ship to Kuwait, and 450 miles via convoy to our desert base in Iraq, ready to accomplish our security mission, with no accidents, injuries, or loss of equipment, all in 21 days.*

When your resume's done, ask a non-military person (not your spouse) to read it to see if he understands it. Then, get it on LinkedIn, Monster, and Career Builder.

Change how you search:

Search the web for companies that hire/assist in the placement/recruiting of former military. Stay in touch with all your military peers and superiors via LinkedIn.com. You may need them as a reference later and you have no idea where they'll be working after they leave the military.

Getting THE Call for Job Interviews and Offers

But, always keep...

- The military *values* you acquired during the time you served
- Your sense of *duty* and *commitment* to something greater than yourself
- Your ability to *make things happen* under difficult circumstances

Focus on your future:

Use the Post 9/11 GI Bill to fund additional education and training (like certifications, licenses, and computer skills like MS Project) that you can add to your resume to make you more marketable. If you don't have a college degree, get one. If you have one, get an MBA. You earned your benefits - now use them!

THE END!

Congratulations! You've reached the end of this book. Thank you for reading! Please remember to share what you have learned with others. If you help others succeed, they'll return the favor.

This book focused on how to Get THE Call for Interviews and Offers.

If you found this book of value, you'll also find value in the other books from *The Effectiveness Guide* series (see Other Books).

You can do this! I have faith in you. What's holding you back?

Self-Assessment:

After reading this book:

- How can you use what you've learned to become more effective tomorrow than you are today?
- How can you use it to become absolutely essential and irreplaceable to any employer?
- How can you use it outside of work (in your community, church, or home) to become better?
- Who else could use it to help them become better?

Do something meaningful with your life. Pay it forward.
Help someone else rise.

ACKNOWLEDGEMENTS

> *"Many people will walk in and out of your life, but only true friends will leave footprints in your heart."*
> - *Eleanor Roosevelt*

I'd like to recognize those with whom I've had the pleasure of serving, whose Leadership and Character I vividly recall, many of whom are not here today to tell their story.

For my military career, I thank Betty McInte, Edward J. Murphy (my Dad), Dale R. Nelson, Geoffrey "Jeff" Prosch, Craig "Randy" Rutler, Dave Wagner, John Andrews, John "The Bear" Warren, John "Jack" Costello, Dan Labin, and Ron Nicholl for their example of Effective Leadership.

To my fellow Brothers and Sisters-in-Arms, I thank you for your faithful service to our nation, especially those who have fallen in the line-of-duty.

Special thanks to my long-time mentor and friend, Joyce Kuntz, who encouraged me to write this book. After leaving the US Military, Joyce was my first and best employer when I joined her consulting firm in Seattle years ago. Joyce is gone now, but her legacy lives on in this book.

> *"I must be able to say with sincerity that to see things differently is a strength, not a weakness, in my relationship with others."*
> - *Joyce Kuntz*

I thank Joyce's husband, Ed Kuntz, who turned out to be the man who brought me to Seattle from Kansas City, to start my incredible second career as an Executive Coach.

For my coaching career, I thank Tony Robbins, Bernard Haldane, Jack Bissell, Len Drew, Wayne McCullum, Bob Schrier, John Hurtig, and Bob Gerberg for their mentoring and coaching.

I thank my Nephew, Rob Chase, for creating the superb cover graphics and his sound advice along the way.

I thank my editors, Adriane Hesselbein, Terri Beard, Lance Revo, Dan Labin, Dennis Cavin, Bill O'Donnell, Andrew Potter, and Kevin Hughes, who did a great job helping me make this book more understandable and useful.

A special thanks to my two dear friends, partners, and co-authors, Lee Lacy and Jason Bowne, who continue to support me in this worthwhile effort.

For all those whose names are not found here, rest assured that you are not forgotten. Your legacy lives on in my heart and in this book because of your immeasurable contributions to my life. This book is for you.

And, finally, I thank my soul-mate and wife, **Diana,** for her love, encouragement and understanding throughout this process.

When I count my blessings, I always count her twice.

ABOUT THE FOUNDER

"I expect to pass through this world but once; any good thing therefore that I can do, or any kindness that I can show to any fellow creature, let me do it now; let me not defer or neglect it, for I shall not pass this way again." - Stephan Grelle

Ed Murphy considers himself lucky. From age 7, he knew what he wanted to be when he grew up. He wanted to be a Soldier. In 1964, four days after graduating from High School, he joined the US Army and found himself in Basic Training and Advanced Infantry Training at Fort Dix, New Jersey.

A year later, Ed became a Cadet at the United States Military Academy at West Point. In 1970, he graduated as a 2d Lieutenant headed to Airborne and Ranger School, then off to Viet Nam for a year.

In 1978, Ed returned to West Point to teach Military Science and earned a Master's Degree from Long Island University in night school. His greatest achievement during his time in the military was helping 1400 soldiers begin their college education during his last two years in West Germany as a Battalion Commander. He wanted to give his soldiers something of real value - something that no one could ever take away. After 23 years as a US Army Officer, from Viet Nam to Desert Storm, he retired in 1993.

Ed then decided, with a little help from *Anthony Robbins*, that his second career would be as an Executive Coach. For the next 21 years, he worked for four of the largest consulting, outplacement and e-cruiting companies in America from Seattle, San Diego, to Kansas City.

In 2012, Ed retired a second time and decided to document everything he learned from those he admired and willingly followed over his 50+ years in both the US Military as an Army Officer and Corporate America as an Executive Coach. Since many of them aren't alive today to tell their stories, he wanted to pay tribute to them before their lessons were lost forever. Thanks to them, he's collected thousands of small and simple things (tactics, techniques, and tools) that have helped and will continue to help future generations to maximize their true career potential by becoming more effective at work and in life.

In 2014, Ed created *TheCAREERMaker.com*, a site dedicated to providing the best-in-class wisdom, knowledge, and advice on how to maximize your true career potential by teaching three simple things; how to become absolutely essential and irreplaceable to any leader, how to become more effective tomorrow than you are today, and how to find and build the career you were meant to have. His greatest joy comes from helping others avoid or overcome the problems he's faced during his lifetime.

In 2016, with the help of two partners and co-authors *Lee O. Lacy and Jason Bowne*, he finally completed *The Effectiveness Guide*, which teaches how to become more effective tomorrow than you are today by consistently producing excellent results; treating others with dignity, respect, and kindness; and helping others to do the same.

Today, Ed considers himself fortunate to get to live in Phoenix, AZ, where he enjoys writing, eating sushi, genealogy, and watching movies with family, friends, and his best friend and wife, *Diana*.

OTHER BOOKS

THESE BOOKS WILL TEACH YOU HOW TO MAXIMIZE YOUR TRUE CAREER POTENTIAL AND ARE AVAILABLE FROM ALL MAJOR ONLINE BOOK RETAILERS

If you liked this book, you'll really like the others in our collection.

From *The Effectiveness Guide* series, topics include:

Volume 1: Your Guide to Better Followership

Volume 2: Your Guide to Better Delegating

Volume 3: Your Guide to Better Planning

Volume 4: Your Guide to Better Organizing

Volume 5: Your Guide to Better Communicating

Volume 6: Your Guide to Better Problem-Solving & Decision-Making

Volume 7: Your Guide to Better Awareness

Volume 8: Your Guide to Better Training

Volume 9: Your Guide to Better Motivating

Volume 10: Your Guide to Better Character

Volume 11: The Effectiveness Guide (includes Volumes 1-10)

Volume 12: Make It Happen! How to Manage Projects

Volume 13: Your Guide to Better Credibility with Your Leader

Discover the Job Searching SECRETS Employer's Don't Want You to Know.

From *The Career Potential* series, topics include:

- Finding a New Job in 90 Days or Less

- Choosing a Career That Matters

- Interview Like You Mean It

- Does Your Resume Make Your Phone Ring?

- Negotiating Total Compensation

- 19+ Proven Ways to Get Your Resume to the Right People

- Changing Your Career?

- Getting THE Call for Job Interviews and Offers

All the above books are also available from our Book Store at *TheCareerMaker.com*.

ONE LAST THING...

Finally, if you feel this information could help someone else, please take a few moments to let them know. If it turns out to make a difference in their life, they'll be forever grateful to you – as will I.

Let's make a difference together – one person at a time!

All the best!

Founder of *TheCAREERMaker.com*
Coauthor of *The Effectiveness Guide*
email: ed.murphy77@gmail.com

Stop wishing you were better and do something about it today!

Discover the Job Searching SECRETS Employer's Don't Want You to Know.

INDEX

30-Second Commercial, 29
Abbreviations, 43
Acronyms, 43
Advertised Job Resume, 50
advertised positions, 70
Alma Mater, 65
Asset Categories, 24
assets, 23
associations, societies and clubs, 66
Band Of Excellence (BOE), 14
Be self-correcting, 93
Behavioral Questions, 84
best compensation, 97
Better use of what, 35
Beyond.com, 54
Body Language, 86
Breaking Bread together, 70
breath is important, 87
buzz-words, 77
Chamber of Commerce, 66
Change how you look, 124
Change how you search, 124
Change how you talk, 123
Change your resume, 124
Close Friends, 68
College Alumni, 65
College Classmates, 65
College Placement Office, 65
Compelling, 39
Contact People I Know (PIK), 58
Contacting companies, 28
conventions, seminars or workshops, 66
Cost of Living Survey, 105
Cover Letter Format, 71
Craigslist, 57
desire, interest, and enthusiasm, 86
DOESN'T GO YOUR WAY, 115
Draft Day, 115
Dress for Success, 86
Ecademy, 57
Emerging Opportunity Letters, 64
Employer's needs, 106
Employment Application?, 108
Executive Search Online, 54
Face-to-face Networking Resume, 50
Family Members, 68
Find a Personal Sponsor, 69
Focus on your future, 125
Focus Statement, 30
Follow up phone call, 94
Format for email, 64

GAMBITS (OR PLAYS)?, 101
getting better over time?, 22
Goals vs. Results, 118
handwritten thank you note, 93
Human Resources, 28
Job Description, 43
Job Fairs, 66
job requisition, 28
Job Search Agent, 55
JobFox, 57
Jobster, 56
Key Performance Indicators (KPIs), 103
Keywords, 42
leave – behind document, 71
Let's Do Lunch, 69
Leverage, 75, 98
liabilities, 23
LinkedIn.com, 56
Major Job Sites, 54
Make more money, 35
Mirroring and Matching, 89
MyWorkster, 57
Negative Questions, 83
Negotiation Meeting, 113
networking cards, 67
Next Step, 92
Offer Letter, 111
PAR STORY, 74
PCF/BOE, 19

PCF/BOE goals, 21
Perceive Value Added, 75
Perceived Value Added, 98
Perception of your Candidacy, 92
Persist and Be Successful, 122
Personal Grooming, 87
Personal questions, 89
PHONE SCREENING INTERVIEW, 75
Plaxo, 56
Positive Cash Flow (or PCF)., 12
Post 9/11 GI Bill, 125
Power of observation, 89
Pre-Emptive Approach, 94
Press On, 122
Private Sector companies, 13
Private Sector Corporations, 11
professional references, 74
Public Sector Organizations, 11, 14
Quick Response (or QR) code, 67
Recruiter Sites, 55
recruiting company, 76
Request, 75
Resume Mailman, 55
ResumeRabbit.com, 54
RULES WHEN NEGOTIATING, 100
Salary Survey, 105
Save money, 35
Search Focus, 30

Search Management System, 117
Seeds of Success Activity Log, 118
Self-Deprecating Comments, 90
Send Advice Letters, 61
Send Approach Letters, 60
Small Business Administration, 12
Social Events, 66
Social Networking Sites, 56
Solve problems today, 36
SPECIAL PURPOSE RESUMES, 50
staffing agencies, 55
Take Massive Action!, 120
Target List, 58
Temporary Employment Sites, 55
Text Only/Plain Text, 51
Total Compensation Package, 98
Track your Communications, 121
transferrable skills, 77
Transferrable Skills, 46
Twitter, 56
US Department of Defense, 15
value added, 20
Visit Target Companies, 62
VisualCV, 57
Web Resume, 50
What improved?, 22
Word of mouth, 28
WordPress Blog, 67
your needs, 106

www.ingramcontent.com/pod-product-compliance
Lightning Source LLC
Chambersburg PA
CBHW061512180526
45171CB00001B/142